AP CALCULUS AB REVIEW

PRACTICE QUESTIONS AND ANSWER EXPLANATIONS

Island Prep Publishing

Copyright 2016 by Island Prep Publishing, Inc.

All rights reserved. No part of this book may be reproduced in any form or by any means without the written permission of the copyright owners.

All brand names and product names referenced in this book are trademarks, registered trademarks, or trade names of their respective holders. Island Prep Publishing Inc. is not associated with any product or vendor in this book.

Published by Island Prep Publishing, Inc., a New York registered company.

All Inquiries should be addressed to:
Island Prep Publishing, Inc.
P.O. Box 1021
Bellmore, NY 11710
info@longislandregentsprep.com

ISBN: 978-1537378497

*AP is a registered trademark of the College Entrance Examination Board. The College Entrance Examination Board is not associated with and does not endorse this book.

External content and images used have been made available under the Creative Commons Attribution 4.0 International Public License.

CONTENTS

Introduction	iii
Questions	1
Limits of Functions	2
Asymptotic and Unbounded Behavior	8
Continuity as a Property of Functions	13
Concept of the Derivative	18
Derivative at a Point	26
Derivative as a Function	40
Second Derivatives	51
Applications of Derivatives	64
Computation of Derivatives	80
The Four Theorems (Extra)	102
Interpretations and Properties of Definite Integrals	108
Applications of Integrals	117
Techniques of Antidifferentiation	127
Applications of Antidifferentiation	132
Numerical Approximations to Definite Integrals	138
Answers	147
Limits of Functions	148
Asymptotic and Unbounded Behavior	150
Continuity as a Property of Functions	153
Concept of the Derivative	156
Derivative at a Point	161
Derivative as a Function	169
Second Derivatives	174
Applications of Derivatives	179
Computation of Derivatives	188
The Four Theorems (Extra)	202
Interpretations and Properties of Definite Integrals	206
Applications of Integrals	212
Techniques of Antidifferentiation	219
Applications of Antidifferentiation	222
Numerical Approximations to Definite Integrals	226

INTRODUCTION

Advanced Placement Calculus AB

Over the past decade, the number of students participating in the Advanced Placement Calculus program has almost doubled, with nearly 300,000 students across the United States taking the AP Calculus AB exam in 2014. This trend is not unique to AP Calculus. In recent years, student participation in the Advanced Placement program has increased in every subject across every demographic. Simply put, students are taking more AP exams in an effort to prepare for and gain admission to selective colleges. This book is designed to help relieve some of the pressure associated these high-stakes courses, and to provide students with the essential strategies, skills, and content to excel on the AP Calculus AB exam.

The AP Calculus AB course is traditionally taken after students have completed algebra, geometry, trigonometry, and pre-calculus, and it is the first calculus course offered at many high schools. The AP Calculus AB course is typically equivalent to one semester of college calculus, and it offers an opportunity for students interested in calculus to earn Advanced Placement credit or exemption from a college-level calculus course. AP Calculus AB topics include the study and application of functions, graphs, and limits, as well as derivatives and integrals. We have used these topics to organize this review book.

The AP Calculus AB exam contains 45 multiple-choice questions and 6 free-response questions. This book, which includes nearly 400 practice questions with detailed explanations, will help students review the essential concepts, topics, and skills to master the AP Calculus AB exam.

QUESTIONS

LIMITS OF FUNCTIONS

DIFFICULTY LEVEL 1

1. Find $\lim\limits_{x \to 0} \dfrac{2x^3 - 10x}{4x - 15x^3}$

   (A) $\dfrac{1}{2}$

   (B) $-\dfrac{5}{2}$

   (C) $-\dfrac{2}{3}$

   (D) $-\dfrac{2}{15}$

   (E) Does not exist

2. If $g(x) = \begin{cases} e^x, & \text{for } x < 3 \\ 5xe^x, & \text{for } x \geq 3 \end{cases}$, then $\lim\limits_{x \to 3} g(x) =$

   (A) e^3
   (B) $15e^3$
   (C) 15
   (D) 3
   (E) Does not exist

3. The graph of the piece-wise function, h(x), is shown below. Which of the statements below is true?

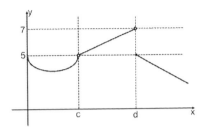

(A) $h(c) = 5$
(B) $h(x)$ is continuous at x = 5
(C) $\lim_{x \to c} h(x) = 5$
(D) $\lim_{x \to d} h(x)$ exists
(E) $h(x)$ is continuous at x = 7

4. If $f(x) = \dfrac{-2x}{x^2 - 16}$, then $\lim_{x \to 4} f(x) =$

(A) ∞
(B) $-\infty$
(C) 0
(D) -8
(E) Does not exist

5. Find $\lim\limits_{x \to \pi} \dfrac{\tan \dfrac{x}{4}}{\ln\left(\dfrac{ex}{\pi}\right)}$

(A) 1
(B) 0
(C) $\dfrac{\sqrt{2}}{2e}$
(D) $\dfrac{\sqrt{2}}{2}$
(E) Does not exist

DIFFICULTY LEVEL 2

6. Find $\lim\limits_{x \to k} \dfrac{x^5 - k^5}{x^{10} - k^{10}}$

(A) $\dfrac{1}{k^5}$
(B) $\dfrac{1}{2k^5}$
(C) $\dfrac{1}{k^{10}}$
(D) 0
(E) Does not exist

7. If $\lim_{x \to 5} f(x) = 3$, then which statements below are _always true_?

   I. f is continuous at x = 5
   II. $\lim_{x \to 5-} f(x) = 3$ and $\lim_{x \to 5+} f(x) = 3$
   III. $f(5) = 3$

   (A) II only
   (B) III only
   (C) I and II
   (D) II and III
   (E) All are true

8. If $g(x) = \dfrac{9-x}{\sqrt{x-3}}$, then $\lim_{x \to 9} g(x) =$

   (A) 6
   (B) -6
   (C) 0
   (D) 3
   (E) Does not exist

9. Find $\lim_{x \to 0} \dfrac{2e^x - 2}{e^{2x} - 1}$

   (A) 2
   (B) 1
   (C) $\dfrac{1}{e}$
   (D) $\dfrac{2}{e}$
   (E) 0

10. The graph of the piece-wise function, f(x), is shown below. Which of the statements below are true?

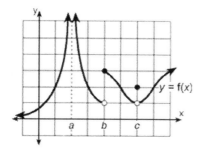

I. $\lim_{x \to b} f(x) = 3$
II. $\lim_{x \to c} f(x) = f(c)$
III. The function is not defined at x = a

(A) III only
(B) I and II
(C) I and III
(D) II and III
(E) None of the statements are true

11. Find $\lim_{x \to 0} \dfrac{(x+3)^3 - 27}{x}$

(A) 27
(B) 54
(C) 1
(D) 0
(E) Does not exist

DIFFICULTY LEVEL 3

12. Find $\lim\limits_{x \to 1} \dfrac{\cot(\pi x)}{\csc(\pi x)}$

    (A) 1
    (B) 0
    (C) $\dfrac{1}{2}$
    (D) −1
    (E) Does not exist

13. Find $\lim\limits_{x \to 5} \dfrac{\dfrac{3}{x} - \dfrac{3}{5}}{x - 5}$

    (A) $\dfrac{3}{25}$
    (B) $-\dfrac{3}{25}$
    (C) $\dfrac{3}{5}$
    (D) $-\dfrac{3}{5}$
    (E) Does not exist

Limits of Functions

ASYMPTOTIC AND UNBOUNDED BEHAVIOR

DIFFICULTY LEVEL 1

1. Find $\lim\limits_{x \to \infty} \dfrac{7x^3 - 10x + 500}{2x^2 + 3x^3}$

    (A) $\dfrac{7}{3}$

    (B) $\dfrac{7}{2}$

    (C) ∞

    (D) 0

    (E) Does not exist

2. Find $\lim\limits_{x \to \infty} \dfrac{x^5 - x + 20}{2x^6 - x^2}$

    (A) $\dfrac{1}{2}$

    (B) ∞

    (C) -1

    (D) 0

    (E) Does not exist

3. If $f(x) = 2^x$, then which line below is a horizontal asymptote to f?

    (A) y = 0

    (B) y = 0.5

    (C) y = 1

    (D) y = 2

    (E) The graph has no horizontal asymptotes

4. Which graph of the equations below has a vertical asymptote at x = 3?

    (A) $y = \dfrac{2x}{2x - 3}$

(B) $y = \dfrac{x^2 - 9}{x - 3}$

(C) $y = \dfrac{4x^2 - 9}{2x - 6}$

(D) $y = \dfrac{3x - 4}{x + 3}$

(E) $y = \dfrac{x - 3}{x + 3}$

5. According to the graph of f below, what is $\lim\limits_{x \to -2+} f(x)$?

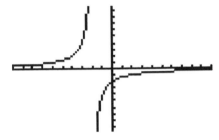

(A) 0
(B) ∞
(C) -∞
(D) 2
(E) Does not exist

DIFFICULTY LEVEL 2

6. Find $\lim\limits_{x \to -\infty} \dfrac{3x^2}{5x-13}$

(A) $\dfrac{3}{5}$

(B) $-\dfrac{3}{13}$

(C) 0

(D) ∞

(E) $-\infty$

7. Find $\lim\limits_{x \to \infty} \dfrac{(1-2x)(x^2+8)}{6x^3-5x^2+12x-10}$

(A) $-\dfrac{1}{3}$

(B) $\dfrac{1}{3}$

(C) 0

(D) $\dfrac{1}{6}$

(E) ∞

8. Which graph of the equations below has no horizontal asymptote?

(A) $y = \dfrac{2x}{x-3}$

(B) $y = \dfrac{2}{x-3}$

(C) $y = \sin x$

(D) $y = \dfrac{\sin x}{x}$

(E) $y = e^{-x}$

9. If the graph of $g(x) = \dfrac{jx+4}{2(x-k)}$ has a vertical asymptote at x = 5 and a horizontal asymptote at y = -1, then the values for j and k are what?
   (A) $j = 2$ and $k = 5$
   (B) $j = -2$ and $k = 5$
   (C) $j = 2$ and $k = -5$
   (D) $j = -1$ and $k = -5$
   (E) $j = 1$ and $k = 5$

10. If the graph of the function shown below is given by the equation, $y = \dfrac{cx^2 + 4}{x^2 + d}$. What is the sum of c and d?

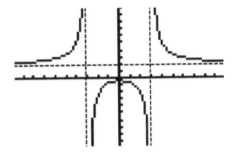

   (A) 9
   (B) -9
   (C) -1
   (D) 5
   (E) -7

11. According to the table of ƒ below, which is an increasing function everywhere, which of the following statements is true about the graph of ƒ?

x	0	.9	.99	1.01	1.1	5	10	100	1000
f(x)	5	1,250	52,625	-52,625	-1,250	-75	-71.125	-70.013	-70.001

(A) A vertical asymptote at x = -70 and a horizontal asymptote at y = 1
(B) A vertical asymptote at x = 1 and a horizontal asymptote at y = -70
(C) A vertical asymptote at x = 1 only
(D) A horizontal asymptote at y = 1 only
(E) A vertical asymptote at x = -70 only

DIFFICULTY LEVEL 3

12. If $g(x) = \dfrac{2e^x + 5}{e^x - 11}$, then which lines below are horizontal asymptotes to g?

(A) y = 0 only
(B) y = 2 only
(C) y = 0 and y = 2
(D) y = 2 and y = $-\dfrac{5}{11}$
(E) y = 0 and y = $-\dfrac{5}{11}$

CONTINUITY AS A PROPERTY OF FUNCTIONS

DIFFICULTY LEVEL 1

1. If g is a continuous function on a closed interval, [2, 8], then which of the following is true?

    (A) g' exists on $(2,8)$
    (B) $\lim_{x \to a} g(x) = g(a)$ for all a in the interval, [2,8]
    (C) For $a < b$ in the interval, [2,8], then $g(a) < g(b)$
    (D) $g'(a) = 0$ for some a in the interval, [2,8]
    (E) None of the above are true

2. Which of the functions below are continuous for all real numbers?

    I. $y = \dfrac{2}{\sin x}$
    II. $y = \sqrt[3]{x}$
    III. $y = e^x$

    (A) None
    (B) II only
    (C) III only
    (D) I and II
    (E) II and III

3. If $\lim_{x \to 3} g(x) = 6$, which of the following must be true?

   (A) g is a continuous function at x = 3
   (B) g is defined at x = 3
   (C) $g(3) = 6$
   (D) g' is defined at x = 3
   (E) None of the above

4. For the graph of $g(x) = \dfrac{x^2 - 7x}{x^2 - 4x - 21}$, what type of discontinuities exist?

   (A) A removable discontinuity at x = -3 and x = 7
   (B) An infinite discontinuity at x = -3 and x = 7
   (C) A removable discontinuity at x = -3 and an infinite discontinuity at x = 7
   (D) An infinite discontinuity at x = -3 and a removable discontinuity at x = 7
   (E) An infinite discontinuity at x = -3 only

5. According to the graph of g below, which of the following statements is false?

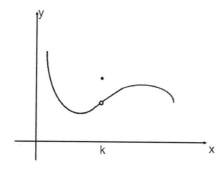

   (A) g is defined at x = k
   (B) $\lim_{x \to k} g(x)$ exists
   (C) g is continuous at x = k
   (D) g has a local maximum at x = k
   (E) k is in the domain of the function g

6. If $f(x) = \begin{cases} \sin(\frac{\pi x}{3}) & \text{for } x < 3 \\ -2 & \text{for } x = 3 \\ 4x - 12 & \text{for } x > 3 \end{cases}$, determine which statements are false.

I. $\lim_{x \to 3-} f(x) = 1$
II. $\lim_{x \to 3+} f(x) = 0$
III. f(3) does not exist

(A) I only
(B) III only
(C) I and III are false
(D) II and III are false
(E) All are false

DIFFICULTY LEVEL 2

7. If $f(x) = \begin{cases} \dfrac{\sqrt{x}-3}{x-9}, & x \neq 9 \\ k & x = 9 \end{cases}$ and if f is continuous at x = 9, then k =

(A) 0
(B) 1
(C) $\dfrac{1}{3}$
(D) 3
(E) $\dfrac{1}{6}$

8. $g(x) = \dfrac{x^3 - 16x}{x-4}$ for all real numbers except x = 4, and g is continuous for all real numbers. Then $g(4) =$

   (A) 32
   (B) 0
   (C) 4
   (D) 8
   (E) 1

9. For the function defined below, at what values is f not continuous?

$$f(x) = \begin{cases} \cos x & x < 0 \\ 1 & 0 \le x < 1 \\ 2 - 3x & 1 \le x < 2 \\ -4\ln(x-1) & x \ge 2 \end{cases}$$

   (A) x = 1 only
   (B) x = 2 only
   (C) x = 0 and x = 1
   (D) x = 1 and x = 2
   (E) x = 0, x = 1, and x = 2

10. For $f(x) = \dfrac{3x}{x-4}$, the function is not continuous at x = 4. The graph of f would be continuous if $f(4) =$

   (A) 0.75
   (B) 0
   (C) -0.75
   (D) 3
   (E) It is not possible for f to be continuous at x = 4

DIFFICULTY LEVEL 3

11. Which of the following functions is continuous, but not differentiable, at x = 0?

    (A) $y = \dfrac{\sin x}{x}$

    (B) $y = \dfrac{1}{\sqrt{x}}$

    (C) $y = \sqrt{x}$

    (D) $y = \sqrt{x^3}$

    (E) $y = e^x$

12. For the function defined by $y = \dfrac{(x-9)^2 (x-1)}{f(x)}$, for what function is y continuous for all real numbers?

    (A) $f(x) = x^2 + 2x - 3$

    (B) $f(x) = (x-9)^2$

    (C) $f(x) = x^2 - 3x$

    (D) $f(x) = x^2 + 9$

    (E) It is not continuous for any of the above functions.

CONCEPT OF THE DERIVATIVE

DIFFICULTY LEVEL 1

1. If $f(x) = 3x + \cos x$, then $f'(x) =$

    (A) $-\sin x$
    (B) $3 - \sin x$
    (C) $3 + \sin x$
    (D) $\sin x$
    (E) $-3x\sin x + 3\cos x$

2. If $g(x) = 2x$, then $g'(7) =$

    (A) 2
    (B) 7
    (C) 1
    (D) 0
    (E) $\dfrac{2}{7}$

3. If $f(x) = 5\sqrt{x} + 3x$, then $f'(4) =$

    (A) $\dfrac{17}{4}$
    (B) 22
    (C) $\dfrac{53}{4}$
    (D) 8
    (E) 17

4. If g is differentiable at x = 3, which of the following are true?

   I. $\lim_{x \to 3} g(x) = g(3)$
   II. g is continuous at x = 3
   III. $g'(3) = 0$

   (A) None of the statements are true
   (B) I only
   (C) II only
   (D) I and II only
   (E) I and III only

5. The graph of the function, f, is shown below on the interval [-2,9]. It has a vertical tangent when x = 1. At what points is the graph continuous, but not differentiable?

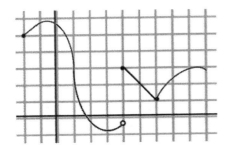

   (A) x = 4 only
   (B) x = 1 and x = 4 only
   (C) x = 1 and x = 6 only
   (D) x = 4 and x = 6 only
   (E) x = 1, x = 4, and x = 6

6. The graph of the function $g(x)=|x-2|$ is shown below. Which of the following statements is false?

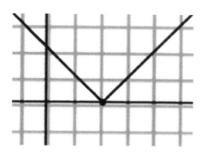

(A) $\lim\limits_{x \to 2} g(x)$ exists
(B) g is continuous at x = 2
(C) g is differentiable at x = 2
(D) $g(2)=0$
(E) None of the above is false

DIFFICULTY LEVEL 2

7. If $h(x)= x^2 +4 -\dfrac{1}{x}$, then $h'(2)=$

(A) 8.25
(B) 7.5
(C) 7.75
(D) 4.25
(E) 3.75

8. If $f(t)=\sqrt[3]{t^4}$, then $f'(8)=$

    (A) 16
    (B) 8
    (C) $\dfrac{14}{3}$
    (D) $\dfrac{2}{3}$
    (E) $\dfrac{8}{3}$

9. Find the instantaneous rate of change of $f(x)=\dfrac{x^4+5x^2+x}{x^2}$ at x = 1

    (A) 13
    (B) 7.5
    (C) 7
    (D) 4
    (E) 1

10. Find the instantaneous rate of change of $f(x)=(x+3)(2x^2-1)$ at x = -1

    (A) 2
    (B) -7
    (C) 17
    (D) -4
    (E) 4

11. If $g(x) = \dfrac{x^2}{2} - \cos x$, then $g'\left(\dfrac{\pi}{6}\right) =$

   (A) $\dfrac{\pi+1}{6}$

   (B) $\dfrac{\pi-3}{6}$

   (C) $\dfrac{\pi+3}{6}$

   (D) $\dfrac{\pi+3\sqrt{3}}{6}$

   (E) $\dfrac{\pi-3\sqrt{3}}{6}$

12. $\dfrac{d}{dx}\left(\dfrac{1}{x^2} + \dfrac{1}{\sqrt{x}}\right)$ at $x = 1$ is

   (A) 2
   (B) 1.5
   (C) 1
   (D) -1.5
   (E) -2.5

13. If g is given by the equation, $g(x) = \sqrt[3]{x}$, which of the following statements are true?

   I. g is continuous at $x = 0$
   II. g is differentiable at $x = 0$
   III. $g'(3) = 0$

   (A) None of the statements are true
   (B) I only
   (C) I and II only
   (D) II and III only
   (E) All of the statements are true

14. If $f(x) = \begin{cases} 8x-10, & x \leq 4 \\ x^2+6, & x > 4 \end{cases}$, then at $x = 4$ the function is

(A) not defined
(B) continuous, but not differentiable
(C) neither continuous nor differentiable
(D) both continuous and differentiable
(E) There is not enough information to determine if f is defined, continuous of differentiable

15. If $f(x) = \log_5 x$, then $f'(2) =$

   (A) $\lim\limits_{h \to 0} \dfrac{\log_5 (x+h)}{h}$

   (B) $\lim\limits_{h \to 0} \dfrac{\log_5 (x+h) - \log_5 2}{h}$

   (C) $\lim\limits_{h \to 0} \dfrac{\log_5 (2+h) - 2}{h}$

   (D) $\lim\limits_{h \to 0} \dfrac{\log_5 (x+h) - \log_5 x}{h}$

   (E) $\lim\limits_{h \to 0} \dfrac{\log_5 (2+h) - \log_5 2}{h}$

16. Find $\lim\limits_{h \to 0} \dfrac{\cos\left(\dfrac{\pi}{6} + h\right) - \cos\dfrac{\pi}{6}}{h}$

   (A) $-\sin x$
   (B) $\dfrac{\sqrt{3}}{2}$
   (C) $-\dfrac{1}{2}$
   (D) $\dfrac{1}{2}$
   (E) $-\dfrac{\sqrt{2}}{2}$

17. What is $\lim\limits_{h \to 0} \dfrac{5(x+h)^2 - 5x^2}{h}$ when x = 3?

(A) Does not exist
(B) 45
(C) 30
(D) $5x^2$
(E) $10x$

18. $\lim\limits_{h \to 0} \dfrac{2\sqrt{x+h} - 2\sqrt{x}}{h} =$

    (A) $\dfrac{\sqrt{x}}{2}$

    (B) $\dfrac{2}{\sqrt{x}}$

    (C) $\dfrac{1}{2\sqrt{x}}$

    (D) $\dfrac{1}{\sqrt{x}}$

    (E) $2\sqrt{x}$

19. If g is a function with $\lim\limits_{h \to 0} \dfrac{g(2+h) - g(2)}{h} = 0$, which of the following statements are true?

    I. g is continuous at $x = 2$
    II. g is differentiable at $x = 2$
    III. $g'(2) = 0$

    (A) II only
    (B) III only
    (C) I and II only
    (D) II and III only
    (E) All of the statements are true

DIFFICULTY LEVEL 3

20. If f is a function with $f(x) = \begin{cases} x^2 + 4x, & x<1 \\ 6x-1, & x\geq 1 \end{cases}$, which of the following statements are true?

   I. f is continuous at $x = 1$
   II. f is differentiable at $x = 1$
   III. $f(x) + x = f'(x)$ when $x = 1$

   (A) None of the statements are true
   (B) I only
   (C) I and II only
   (D) I and III only
   (E) All of the statements are true

21. Given $f(x) = \begin{cases} 2x^2 + 5x + a, & x<1 \\ bx-3, & x\geq 1 \end{cases}$, which is differentiable at $x = 1$. Also, a and b are constants. Find $(a+b)$.

   (A) 8
   (B) 10
   (C) -10
   (D) -15
   (E) -16

DERIVATIVE AT A POINT

DIFFICULTY LEVEL 1

1. Find $f'(8)$, when $f(x) = \sqrt[3]{x^2} - e^2$

   (A) $\dfrac{8}{3} - e^2$

   (B) $\dfrac{8}{3}$

   (C) $\dfrac{8}{3} - 2e$

   (D) $2 - 2e$

   (E) $\dfrac{3}{2}$

2. For the functions f and g, such that $f(x) = x^3 - 2$ and the derivative of g is $g'(x) = 15x + 18$, at which x-value in the First Quadrant are the tangent lines to the graphs of each function parallel?

   (A) 1
   (B) 2
   (C) $\sqrt{5}$
   (D) 3
   (E) 6

3. If $g(x) = \arctan x$, then $g'(1) =$

   (A) $\dfrac{\pi}{4}$

   (B) $\dfrac{1}{2}$

   (C) 0

   (D) $\dfrac{1}{\cos^2 1}$

   (E) Does not exist

4. The graph of the curve given by $y^2 = 2 + xy$ has a derivative of $\dfrac{dy}{dx} = \dfrac{y}{2y - x}$. Find all points on the curve where the tangent line is horizontal.

   (A) $(-4, 0)$

   (B) $(0, 0)$

   (C) $(0, \pm\sqrt{2})$

   (D) $(2, 1)$

   (E) The tangent line to the curve is never horizontal

5. Consider the curve given by $y^2 + 2x^2 = 16$, and its derivative, $\dfrac{dy}{dx} = -\dfrac{2x}{y}$. Find all points on the curve where the tangent line is horizontal.

   (A) $(0, 4)$

   (B) $(0, 4) \text{ and} (0, -4)$

   (C) $(2\sqrt{2}, 0)$

   (D) $(2\sqrt{2}, 0) \text{ and} (-2\sqrt{2}, 0)$

   (E) The tangent line to the curve is never horizontal

6. Consider the curve given by $y^2 + 2x^2 = 16$, and its derivative, $\dfrac{dy}{dx} = -\dfrac{2x}{y}$. Find all points on the curve where the tangent line is vertical.

(A) $(0,4)$
(B) $(0,4)$ and $(0,-4)$
(C) $(2\sqrt{2},0)$
(D) $(2\sqrt{2},0)$ and $(-2\sqrt{2},0)$
(E) The tangent line to the curve is never vertical

7. An equation of the tangent line to the graph of $y = 2x + \sin x$ at the point $(\pi, 2\pi)$ is

(A) $y = x$
(B) $y = x + \pi$
(C) $y = 3x - \pi$
(D) $y = x - \pi$
(E) $y = x + 2\pi$

8. Let f be a differentiable function such that $f(2) = 7$ and $f'(2) = 4$. Using the tangent line to the graph of f at 2, approximate the value of $f(2.1)$.

(A) 23.4
(B) 9.4
(C) 7.4
(D) 6.6
(E) 0.775

DIFFICULTY LEVEL 2

9. Find the slope of the function, $f(x) = \cos^2(x)$, when $x = \dfrac{\pi}{3}$.

   (A) $-\dfrac{\sqrt{3}}{2}$

   (B) $-\dfrac{\sqrt{3}}{4}$

   (C) 1

   (D) $-\dfrac{3}{4}$

   (E) $\dfrac{3}{4}$

10. The slope of the tangent line to the graph of $g(x) = \ln(4x-2)$ at $x = 1$ is

    (A) 4
    (B) 2
    (C) 1
    (D) $\dfrac{1}{2}$
    (E) Undefined

11. If the graph of the function, $h(x) = x^2 + 3x + a$ is tangent to the line $2y + 6x = 0$, find a.

    (A) -3
    (B) 0
    (C) 3
    (D) 9
    (E) 18

Derivative at a Point

12. The graph of the function, $y = \dfrac{4x^3}{3} - 6x^2 - x + 5$ is tangent to the line y + x = k, where k is a constant. What are the possible values of k?

    (A) 0 and 5
    (B) 5 and -13
    (C) 0 and 3
    (D) 5 and -16
    (E) 0 only

13. At what point on the graph of $f(x) = \dfrac{x^2}{4}$ is the tangent line parallel to $2y - 3x = 4$?

    (A) $\left(\dfrac{3}{2}, \dfrac{9}{16}\right)$

    (B) $\left(3, \dfrac{13}{2}\right)$

    (C) $\left(3, \dfrac{9}{4}\right)$

    (D) $\left(\dfrac{3}{2}, \dfrac{17}{4}\right)$

    (E) $\left(3, \dfrac{3}{2}\right)$

14. If $f(x) = e^{2x-2}$, find the x-value such that $f'(x) = 2e$.

    (A) $\dfrac{3}{2}$
    (B) 1
    (C) $\dfrac{3 + \ln 2}{2}$
    (D) 3
    (E) 0

15. The instantaneous rate of change of $g(x) = \ln(3x^2)$ at $x = e$ is

(A) $\dfrac{2}{e^2}$

(B) 6

(C) $\dfrac{1}{e}$

(D) $\dfrac{1}{3e^2}$

(E) $\dfrac{2}{e}$

16. The graph of the curve given by $y^2 = 2 + xy$ has a derivative of $\dfrac{dy}{dx} = \dfrac{y}{2y - x}$. Find all points on the curve where the tangent line has a slope of $\dfrac{1}{4}$.

(A) $(6, 1)$

(B) $(0, 0)$

(C) $(0, \pm\sqrt{2})$

(D) $(-1, 1)$

(E) The tangent line to the curve never has a slope of $\dfrac{1}{4}$

Derivative at a Point

17. The graph of the function, f', the derivative of f is shown below on the interval [-3,7]. It has a vertical tangent when x = 1. For which x-values will the graph of f have horizontal tangent lines?

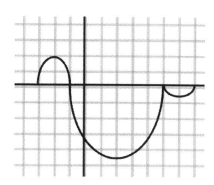

(A) x = -1 only
(B) x = 5 only
(C) x = -2, x = 2, and x = 6
(D) x = -3, x = -1, and x = 7
(E) x = -3, x = -1, x = 5, and x = 7

18. If $6x^2 + y^2 = 2xy + 20$ is the equation of a curve, its derivative is given by $\dfrac{dy}{dx} = \dfrac{y - 6x}{y - x}$. At which points is the tangent line to the curve vertical?

I. (-2, -2)
II. (1, 1)
III. (2, 2)

(A) II only
(B) III only
(C) I and III only
(D) II and III only
(E) At all three points

19. If $6x^2 + y^2 = 2xy + 30$ is the equation of a curve, its derivative is given by $\dfrac{dy}{dx} = \dfrac{y-6x}{y-x}$.

    At which points is the tangent line to the curve horizontal?

    I. (-2, -12)
    II. (0, 0)
    III. (1, 6)

    (A) I only
    (B) II only
    (C) III only
    (D) I and III only
    (E) II and III only

20. If $f(x) = e^{2x} - 3x$, find the equation of the tangent line of f at x = 0.

    (A) $y = -3x$
    (B) $y + 1 = x$
    (C) $y + 1 = -1x$
    (D) $y - 1 = -1x$
    (E) $y - 1 = -2x$

21. If $f(x) = 2 + \tan(\pi x)$, find the equation of the tangent line of f at x = 1.

    (A) $y - 2 = \pi(x - 1)$
    (B) $y - 2 = -\pi(x - 1)$
    (C) $y - 2 = (2 + \pi)(x - 1)$
    (D) $y - 2 = 1(x - 1)$
    (E) $y - 3 = 1(x - 1)$

Derivative at a Point

22. For the function $y = \ln(x^2)$, find the equation of the tangent line of y at $x = 1$.

   (A) $y - 1 = 2(x - 1)$
   (B) $y = x$
   (C) $y = 2(x - 1)$
   (D) $y = x - 1$
   (E) $y = -2(x - 1)$

23. Given the function $f(x) = 3x^3 - 3x$, which of the equations below are tangent to the graph of f at the point where $f'(x) = 6$?

   I. $y = 6x + 6$
   II. $y = 6x - 6$
   III. $y = 6x + 1$

   (A) I only
   (B) II only
   (C) III only
   (D) I and II only
   (E) I and III only

24. An equation of the tangent line to the graph of $y = \dfrac{3x - 1}{2x + 2}$ at the point $\left(0, -\dfrac{1}{2}\right)$ is

   (A) $y - \dfrac{1}{2} = 2x$
   (B) $y - \dfrac{1}{2} = x$
   (C) $y + \dfrac{1}{2} = -2x$
   (D) $y + \dfrac{1}{2} = x$
   (E) $y + \dfrac{1}{2} = 2x$

25. An equation of the line normal to the graph of $y = 3x^2 - 5x$ at $x = -1$ is

   (A) $y - 2 = -1(x - 1)$

(B) $y-8=11(x+1)$

(C) $y-8=\dfrac{1}{11}(x+1)$

(D) $y-8=-\dfrac{1}{11}(x+1)$

(E) $y-2=(x-1)$

26. For the function g, $g(-1)=3$ and $g'(x)=5x+7$. What is the approximation for $g(-1.1)$ found by using the tangent line to the graph of g at x = -1.1?

   (A) 2.9
   (B) 2.8
   (C) 1.8
   (D) 1.5
   (E) -22.2

27. Let f be a differentiable function such that $f(2)=-3$ and $f'(2)=-2.5$. Using the tangent line to the graph of f at 2, approximate the zero of f.

   (A) 3.2
   (B) 2.0
   (C) 0.8
   (D) -2.0
   (E) -3.2

28. Using linear approximation, estimate the value of $f(4.4)$, if $f(x)=\sqrt{x}$.

   (A) 2.05
   (B) 2.1
   (C) 2.2
   (D) 2.35
   (E) 2.4

29. Values for a decreasing, differentiable function, f, are given in the table below. Using the given data, what is the best approximate value for $f'(3)$?

Derivative at a Point

x	1	2	3	4	5
f(x)	70	40	25	18	14

(A) -7

(B) -11

(C) -20

(D) 14

(E) 25

DIFFICULTY LEVEL 3

30. If $xy + y^2 = 12$ is the equation of a curve, its derivative is given by $\dfrac{dy}{dx} = \dfrac{y}{4y - x}$. Which of the following are true statements?

   I.   The curve has no horizontal tangents

   II. When x = 4, the curve has two possible tangent lines with a slope of $-\dfrac{1}{4}$ and $-\dfrac{3}{4}$

   III. The curve has no vertical tangents

   (A) I only

   (B) III only

   (C) I and II only

   (D) I and III only

   (E) All of the statements are true

31. If the graph of a curve is given by $y(2x^2 + 2) = 16$, how many horizontal and vertical tangent lines does the graph of the curve have?

    (A) 1 Horizontal, 0 Vertical
    (B) 2 Horizontal, 0 Vertical
    (C) 1 Horizontal, 1 Vertical
    (D) 1 Horizontal, 2 Vertical
    (E) 2 Horizontal, 2 Vertical

32. For the function $h(x) = xf(x)$, where $f(-1) = 3$ and $f'(-1) = -5$, find the equation of the tangent line of h at x = -1.

    (A) $y - 3 = -5(x + 1)$
    (B) $y + 3 = 5(x + 1)$
    (C) $y + 3 = 5(x + 1)$
    (D) $y - 3 = 8(x - 1)$
    (E) $y + 3 = 8(x + 1)$

33. An equation of the tangent line to the graph of $y = (2 - x)^2 x$ at the point $(1, 1)$ is

    (A) $y = -3x + 4$
    (B) $y = 3x - 2$
    (C) $y = 2x - 1$
    (D) $y = -x + 2$
    (E) $y = x$

34. Consider the curve defined by $y + \sin y = x + 2$ for $0 \leq y \leq 2\pi$. What is the equation of the vertical tangent line to the curve?

    (A) $x = \pi - 2$
    (B) $x = \pi - 1$
    (C) $x = \pi$
    (D) $x = \pi + 1$
    (E) $x = \pi + 2$

Derivative at a Point

35. For the function $g(x) = 2\sin^2 x + \cos x$, what is the equation of the normal line of g at $x = \dfrac{\pi}{3}$?

(A) $y - 2 = -\dfrac{2\sqrt{3}}{3}(x - \dfrac{\pi}{3})$

(B) $y - \dfrac{1+\sqrt{3}}{2} = \dfrac{-1+2\sqrt{3}}{2}(x - \dfrac{\pi}{3})$

(C) $y - 2 = \dfrac{\sqrt{3}}{2}(x - \dfrac{\pi}{3})$

(D) $y - \dfrac{1+\sqrt{3}}{2} = \dfrac{-2}{-1+2\sqrt{3}}(x - \dfrac{\pi}{3})$

(E) $y - 2 = -\dfrac{2\sqrt{3}}{9}(x - \dfrac{\pi}{3})$

36. The slope of the normal line to $y = \ln(\cos x)$ at $x = \pi$ is

(A) 0

(B) 1

(C) -1

(D) $-\dfrac{1}{\pi}$

(E) Undefined

37. For the function $h(x) = e^{2x} + f(x)$, where $f(0) = 3$ and $f'(0) = -5$, find the equation of the normal line of h at $x = -1$.

(A) $y = -5x + 3$

(B) $y = \dfrac{1}{5}x + 3$

(C) $y = -3x + 4$

(D) $y = \dfrac{1}{3}x + 4$

(E) $y = \dfrac{1}{3}x + \dfrac{4}{3}$

38. Let *f* be a twice differentiable function such that $f(2)=1$ *and* $f'(2)=-2$. Using the tangent line at x = 2, for what number k, is the approximation of $f(k)$ equal to k?

(A) 1.67
(B) 2.33
(C) 2.5
(D) 5.0
(E) -1.0

39. A shark tracked by a GPS tag sends its distance from the station every hour. The differentiable function *P* is the shark's position from the station in kilometers. The table below gives the data for the shark during the first 4 hours. If the shark's distance and velocity, *P'*, moving away from the station are always increasing during the first 4 hours, which of the following values could be its approximate position at t = 3.5 hours?

t	2	3	4
P(t)	15km	45km	80km

I. 52.5km
II. 55km
III. 70km
IV. 75km

(A) All four are possible
(B) II only
(C) III only
(D) II and III only
(E) I, II, and III only

DERIVATIVE AS A FUNCTION

DIFFICULTY LEVEL 1

1. The function $g(x) = 2x^3 - 4x^2$ has a local minimum. At what x-value is this minimum?
   - (A) 2
   - (B) 0
   - (C) $\dfrac{4}{3}$
   - (D) $-\dfrac{4}{3}$
   - (E) $\dfrac{8}{3}$

2. The function $f(x) = 2x^3 - x^2$ is defined for all real numbers. On which of the following intervals is f increasing?
   - (A) $-\infty < x < -0.5$
   - (B) $-0.5 < x < 0$
   - (C) $0 < x < 0.5$
   - (D) $0 < x < \infty$
   - (E) f is never increasing

3. If $g(x) = 3x^3 - 18$, then at what x-value is the relative maximum of g?
   - (A) $\sqrt[3]{6}$
   - (B) 0
   - (C) $\sqrt{2}$
   - (D) $-\sqrt{2}$
   - (E) g has no maximum

4. The function $h(x)$ is differentiable for all real numbers. The graph of h has a relative maximum at x = 2 and a relative minimum at x = 5, but no other relative extrema. Which of the following statements must be true?

   (A) $h'(1)$ is negative
   (B) $h'(3)$ is positive
   (C) $h'(2) > h'(5)$
   (D) h is decreasing over the interval (2, 5)
   (E) h is increasing over the interval (2, 5)

5. The function $f(x) = -2x^3 + 24x - 6$ is given. On what open intervals is the graph of f decreasing?

   (A) $(-\infty, -2)$ only
   (B) $(2, \infty)$ only
   (C) $(-\infty, -2)$ and $(2, \infty)$
   (D) $(-2, 2)$ only
   (E) h is never decreasing

6. The derivative f' of a function is continuous and has only two zeroes, as indicated in the table below. f and f' are defined for all real numbers. On which interval is f increasing?

x	0	1	2	3	4	5	6
f'(x)	-4	-6	0	2	1	0	-4

   (A) $0 < x < 2$ and $5 < x < 6$
   (B) $2 < x < 3$ only
   (C) $2 < x < 5$
   (D) $0 < x < 3$
   (E) $3 < x < 6$

7. The graph of f', the derivative of f, is shown below on the interval [-2,10]. At what x-values of x does f have relative minimums for $-2 < x < 10$?

41

Derivative as a Function

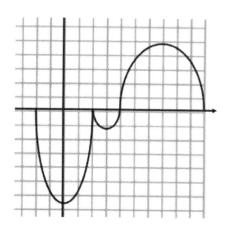

(A) x = 0 only
(B) x = 7 only
(C) x = 0 and x = 3
(D) x = 2 and x = 4
(E) x = 4 only

8. The graph of f′, the derivative of f, is shown below on the interval [-5,3.5]. What are all of the intervals on which the graph of f is decreasing?

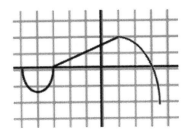

(A) $(-5,-4)$ and $(3,3.5)$
(B) $(-5,-3)$ and $(3,3.5)$
(C) $(-5,-4)$ and $(1,3.5)$
(D) $(1,3)$
(E) $(-4,-3)$

9. If f is a continuous function such that $f'(x) > 0$ for all except at $x = 0$. $f'(0)$ is undefined. Which of the following could be the graph of f?

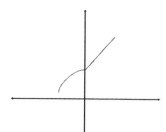

I.

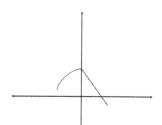

II.

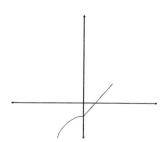

III.

(A) I only
(B) II only
(C) III only
(D) I and II
(E) I and III

DIFFICULTY LEVEL 2

10. If $f(x)=(x^2-90)(2x+3)$, for what values of x does f have a relative maximum?

    (A) 5
    (B) -6
    (C) $\sqrt{90}$
    (D) 0
    (E) $-\dfrac{3}{2}$

11. If $f(x)=(x-1)(x-2)^2(x-3)(x-4)^3$, how many relative maximums does the graph of f have?

    (A) 0
    (B) 1
    (C) 2
    (D) 3
    (E) 4

12. If $\dfrac{dy}{dx}=x(x-3)^2(x-6)$, then the graph of y has which of the following relative extrema?

    I. A relative maximum at x = 0
    II. A relative minimum at x = 3
    III. A relative maximum at x = 6

    (A) I only
    (B) III only
    (C) I and III only
    (D) II and III only
    (E) I, II, and III

13. The function h is defined such that $h(x)<0$ for all real numbers, and h is always increasing. If $f(x) = (x^2)h(x)$, then which of the following statements must be true?

    (A) f has a maximum at $x = 0$
    (B) f has a minimum at $x = 0$
    (C) $f'(0)$ does not exist
    (D) f is increasing for $x < 0$
    (E) f is decreasing for $x < 0$

14. The function $f(x) = xe^x$ is defined for all real numbers. On what open intervals is the graph of f increasing?

    (A) $(-\infty, -1)$
    (B) $(-1, \infty)$
    (C) $(-1, 0)$ only
    (D) f is always increasing
    (E) f is never increasing

15. At $x = 1$, which of the following statements is true about the function $g(x) = x^2 \ln(x)$?

    (A) g is decreasing
    (B) g is increasing
    (C) g has a relative minimum
    (D) g has a relative maximum
    (E) g is undefined

16. Given $f'(x) = \dfrac{|x^2 + 3x - 10|}{x+1}$. It is the derivative of f, which is defined for all real numbers. Then f is increasing on the interval

   (A) $(-\infty, -5)$ only
   (B) $(-\infty, -1)$
   (C) $(-5, 2)$
   (D) $(2, \infty)$
   (E) $(-\infty, \infty)$

17. The function f is defined for $-3 \leq x \leq 7$. Its continuous derivative, f', is shown below. Which of the following statements is false?

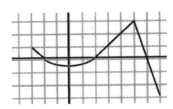

   (A) f has a local maximum at x = -2 and x = 6
   (B) f has a local minimum at x = 2
   (C) f is increasing from $(0, 5)$
   (D) f is decreasing from $(-2, 2)$ and $(4, 5)$
   (E) $f'(5)$ exists

18. The graph of the derivative of *f* is shown below. Which of the following graphs below could be the graph of *f*?

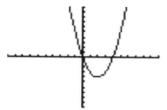

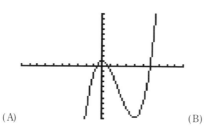

(A)   (B)

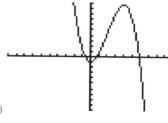

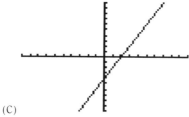

(C)   (D)

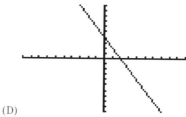

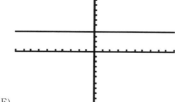

(E)

19. The graph of the f is shown below. Which of the following graphs below could be the graph of $f'(x)$?

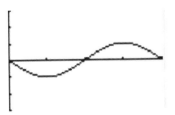

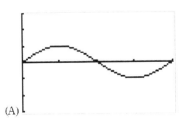
(A)

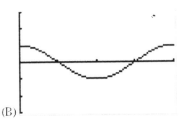
(B)

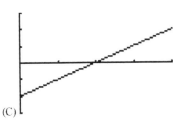
(C)

(D)

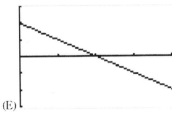
(E)

DIFFICULTY LEVEL 3

20. For the function $h(x) = |x^2 - 4x - 5|$, what is the maximum value of h on the interval [-1, 6]?

    (A) 0
    (B) 2
    (C) 7
    (D) 9
    (E) 12

21. The function h is defined by $h(x) = f(x) - 3x$, and the graph of f' is included below. For what x-values is the graph of h decreasing?

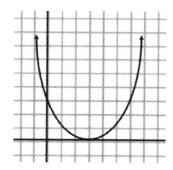

    (A) $0 < x < 6$
    (B) $-\infty < x < 0$ only $6 < x < \infty$
    (C) $-\infty < x < 3$
    (D) h is never decreasing
    (E) h is always decreasing

SECOND DERIVATIVES

DIFFICULTY LEVEL 1

1. The function $f(x) = 3x^4 - \dfrac{9x^2}{2} + 6x$, is defined for all real numbers. On which of the following intervals is f concave up?
   (A) $-\infty < x < -0.5$ only
   (B) $0.5 < x < \infty$ only
   (C) $-\infty < x < -0.5$ and $0.5 < x < \infty$
   (D) $-0.5 < x < 0.5$
   (E) $x > 0$

2. If $f''(x) = -2x^2(x+2)(x-3)$, the graph of f has points of inflection at
   (A) x = 0 only
   (B) x = -2 only
   (C) x = -2 and x = 3 only
   (D) x = 0 and x = 3 only
   (E) x = -2, x = 0, and x = 3

3. For the differentiable function f, the second derivative f'' has selected values in the table below. f and f'' are defined for all real numbers. The graph of f has at least how many points of inflection?

x	0	1	2	3	4	5	6
f''(x)	5.5	0	-3	-3	1.5	0	-2

   (A) 1
   (B) 2
   (C) 3
   (D) 4
   (E) 0

51

4. The graph of f is shown below on the interval [-2,10]. For what intervals is the graph of f concave up?

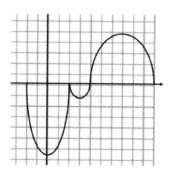

(A) $(-2,2)$ and $(2,4)$
(B) $(0,2)$ and $(3,4)$ only
(C) $(4,10)$
(D) $(4,7)$ only
(E) $(7,10)$ only

5. The graph of f is shown below. f is a twice differentiable function. Which of the following statements is true?

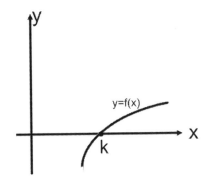

(A) $f''(k) < f'(k) < f(k)$
(B) $f''(k) < f(k) < f'(k)$
(C) $f'(k) < f''(k) < f(k)$
(D) $f'(k) < f(k) < f''(k)$
(E) $f(k) < f'(k) < f''(k)$

6. If y is a function of x such that y' changes sign once and y'' does not change sign over the domain of y, which of the following below could be a graph of y?

(A)

(B)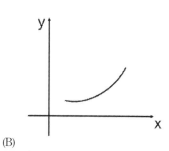

(C)

(D)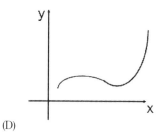

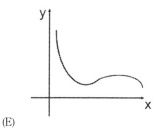

(E)

DIFFICULTY LEVEL 2

7. The function $f(x) = \dfrac{9x^5}{5} - 6x^4 + 6x^3 + \dfrac{1}{5}$ has a point of inflection at

   (A) $(-1, \dfrac{-68}{5})$ only

   (B) $(-1, \dfrac{-68}{5})$ and $(0, \dfrac{1}{5})$

   (C) $(0, \dfrac{1}{5})$ and $(1, 2)$

   (D) $(1, 2)$ only

   (E) $(0, \dfrac{1}{5})$ only

8. The graph of $y = -\cos x - \dfrac{x^2}{4}$ for $0 \leq x < 2\pi$, is concave down when

   (A) $\dfrac{\pi}{3} < x < \dfrac{5\pi}{3}$

   (B) $\dfrac{\pi}{6} < x < \dfrac{5\pi}{6}$

   (C) $0 < x < \dfrac{\pi}{3}$ and $\dfrac{5\pi}{3} < x < 2\pi$

   (D) $0 < x < \dfrac{\pi}{6}$ and $\dfrac{5\pi}{6} < x < 2\pi$

   (E) The graph of y is never concave down

Second Derivatives

9. If $\dfrac{d^2 y}{dx^2} = 3^{-x}(2-x)^3$, then which of the following are true?

   I. y has no points of inflection
   II. y is concave down in the interval $(2, \infty)$
   III. $\dfrac{d^2 y}{dx^2}(1) = -3$

   (A) I only
   (B) II only
   (C) III only
   (D) I and II only
   (E) II and III

10. At what x-value does the graph of $f(x) = \dfrac{1}{x} + \dfrac{2}{x^2}$ have a point of inflection?

    (A) 0
    (B) -4
    (C) -6
    (D) 2
    (E) There are no points of inflection

11. The derivative of the function y, which is defined everywhere except x = 0, is $\dfrac{dy}{dx} = \dfrac{e^x}{2x^2}$. Which of the following statements is true?

    (A) y has points of inflection at x = 0 and x = 2
    (B) y has a point of inflection at x = 0 only
    (C) y has a point of inflection at x = 2 only
    (D) y has points of inflection at x = 1 and x = 2
    (E) y has no points of inflection

12. Find the equation of the tangent line to the graph of $g(x) = 2x^3 - 6x^2$ at its point of inflection.

   (A) $y = -6x + 2$
   (B) $y = 18x + 10$
   (C) $y = 6x - 10$
   (D) $y = -2x + 6$
   (E) $y = -8$

13. For the graph given by the equation $f(x) = 2x^2 - \ln(x)$ is defined for all $x > 0$. What is the slope of the normal to the tangent line at its point of inflection?

   (A) 0
   (B) 1
   (C) $\dfrac{15}{2}$
   (D) $-\dfrac{2}{15}$
   (E) Undefined

14. The graph of f′, the derivative of f, is shown below on the interval [1,9]. What are all of the intervals on which the graph of f is concave up?

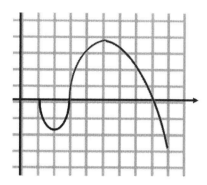

(A) $1 < x < 3$
(B) $2 < x < 3$ only
(C) $3 < x < 8$
(D) $3 < x < 5$ only
(E) $2 < x < 5$

15. The function f is defined for $-3 \leq x \leq 7$. Its continuous second derivative, f'', is shown below. On which interval is f' increasing?

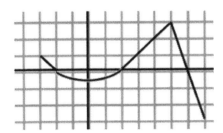

(A) $2 < x < 5$ only
(B) $-3 < x < -2$ and $2 < x < 6$
(C) $0 < x < 5$
(D) $2 < x < 5$ only
(E) $-2 < x < 2$ and $6 < x < 7$

16. The graph of the f'', the second derivative of f, is shown at right. Which of the following graphs below could be the graph of f?

(A)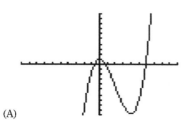
(B)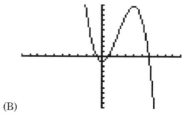

(C)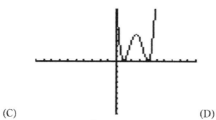
(D)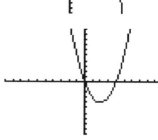

(E)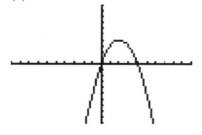

17. The graph of the *f* is shown at right. Which of the following graphs below could be the graph of $f''(x)$?

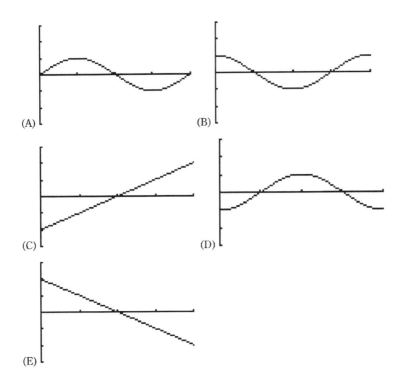

18. The graph of the function $f(x)$ is shown below with $1 \le x \le 4$. For which interval below is $f' < 0$ and $f'' < 0$?

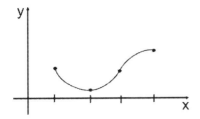

(A) $1 < x < 2$
(B) $2 < x < 3$
(C) $3 < x < 4$
(D) $1 < x < 2$ and $2 < x < 3$
(E) The graph of f never has $f' < 0$ and $f'' < 0$

DIFFICULTY LEVEL 3

19. The graph of $f(x) = \dfrac{3}{4-x}$ is given. Where is the graph of f concave up?

(A) $x > 0$
(B) $x < 0$
(C) $x > 4$
(D) $x < 4$
(E) $x < 6$

20. The function f is defined by $f(x) = \cos(ax)$, where a is an unknown such that $0 \le a < 2\pi$. If f has a point of inflection at $x = 1$, then $f''(0) =$

(A) 0
(B) $\dfrac{\pi^2}{2}$
(C) $-\dfrac{\pi^2}{2}$
(D) $\dfrac{\pi^2}{4}$
(E) $-\dfrac{\pi^2}{4}$

21. The function g is defined on the interval (-1, 9). It has a derivative defined by $g'(x) = (f(x))^2$, and the graph of f is included below. Which of the statements below is true?

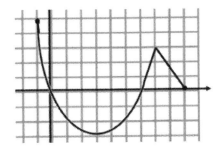

(A) At $x = 0$, g is concave up
(B) At $x = 1$, g is concave up
(C) At $x = 3$, g is concave up
(D) At $x = 5$, g is concave up
(E) At $x = 8$, g is concave up

APPLICATIONS OF DERIVATIVES

DIFFICULTY LEVEL 1

1. The sides of a square, s, are increasing at a rate given by $\frac{ds}{dt} = 2 cm/\min$. At the instant that the sides of the square are 5cm, what is the rate of change of the area of the square?

   (A) $2 cm^2/\min$
   (B) $4 cm^2/\min$
   (C) $10 cm^2/\min$
   (D) $20 cm^2/\min$
   (E) $25 cm^2/\min$

2. At a moment in time, the area of a circle is expanding twice as fast as the diameter of the circle. What is the radius at this moment?

   (A) $\frac{1}{\pi}$
   (B) 1
   (C) $\frac{2}{\pi}$
   (D) 2
   (E) π

3. Let g be a differentiable function such that $g(2) = 9$, $g(-3) = 2$, $g'(2) = 11$, $g'(-3) = 6$. The function g has an inverse function, $g^{-1}(x)$ for all x. What is $(g^{-1})'(2)$?

   (A) $\dfrac{1}{6}$

   (B) $\dfrac{1}{11}$

   (C) $\dfrac{1}{2}$

   (D) $-\dfrac{1}{3}$

   (E) The value does not exist

4. Let f be the function defined by $f(x) = 4x^3 + 18x - 50$. If $g(x) = f^{-1}(x)$ and $g(18) = 2$, what is the value of $g'(18)$?

   (A) $\dfrac{1}{66}$

   (B) $-\dfrac{1}{18}$

   (C) $\dfrac{2}{33}$

   (D) $-\dfrac{1}{72}$

   (E) The value does not exist

5. If $f(x) = x^5 + x^3 - 1$ and $g(x) = f^{-1}(x)$, what is the value of $g'(-3)$?

   (A) -8
   (B) -1
   (C) $\dfrac{1}{8}$
   (D) $-\dfrac{1}{2}$
   (E) $\dfrac{1}{432}$

6. A particle moves along the x-axis such that its position is given by $p(t) = 2t^2 - 10t + 12$ where t is time. At what value of t is the velocity of the particle zero?

   (A) 0
   (B) 1.5
   (C) 2
   (D) 2.5
   (E) 3

7. The position of a laser scanning a document is given by $p(t) = \dfrac{t^4}{2} - \dfrac{16t^3}{3} + 16t^2 - 6$ where t is time. For what times is the laser at rest?

   (A) 0 only
   (B) 0 and 2
   (C) 2 only
   (D) 4 only
   (E) 0 and 4

8. A particle moves along the x-axis such that its position is given by $p(t) = \dfrac{t^3}{6} - 2t^2 + 6t + 2$ where $0 \le t \le 10$ is time. During which intervals is the particle moving to the right?

   (A) $(0,2)$ only
   (B) $(0,2)$ and $(6,10)$
   (C) $(2,6)$ only
   (D) $(4,10)$ only
   (E) $(2,4)$ and $(6,10)$

9. Find the average velocity of a particle from $0 \leq t \leq 2$, if the position of the particle is given by $p(t) = -1 - t^3$.

   (A) -1
   (B) -2
   (C) -3
   (D) -4
   (E) -5

10. The graph below shows the velocity of a particle moving along a straight line from 1 to 9 seconds. At what times is the acceleration of the particle negative?

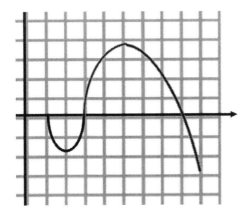

   (A) $1 < t < 3$ and $8 < t < 9$
   (B) $1 < t < 2$ and $5 < t < 8$
   (C) $1 < t < 2$ and $5 < t < 9$
   (D) $1 < t < 2$ and $8 < t < 9$
   (E) $2 < t < 3$ and $5 < t < 8$

11. The graph below shows the velocity of a fish swimming in a river, for $0 < t < 10$ where t is time in seconds. At what time does the fish change directions in the river?

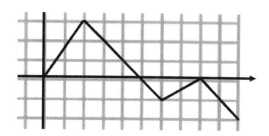

(A) 2 and 6 seconds
(B) 2, 6, and 8 seconds
(C) 6 and 8 seconds
(D) 5 seconds only
(E) 8 seconds only

DIFFICULTY LEVEL 2

12. The sides of a rectangle, x and y, are each changing over time. x is increasing at a rate of $3 in/\sec$, and y is decreasing at a rate of $1 in/\sec$. When both x and y are 7in, $\dfrac{dA}{dt} =$

(A) $-3 in^2/\sec$
(B) $3 in^2/\sec$
(C) $14 in^2/\sec$
(D) $28 in^2/\sec$
(E) $49 in^2/\sec$

13. The formula for the volume of a sphere is $V = \dfrac{4}{3}\pi r^3$ and the formula for the surface area of a sphere is $A = 4\pi r^2$. The rate of change of the sphere is given by $\dfrac{dr}{dt} = 1$. At one

moment, the rate of change of the volume equals the rate of change of the surface area. Find the radius of the sphere at that moment.

(A) 0.5
(B) 1
(C) $\sqrt{2}$
(D) 2
(E) 4

14. A spherical snowball, which is rolling down a hillside, has a volume given by $V = \frac{4}{3}\pi r^3$. When the radius of the snowball is $\sqrt{3}$ ft, the volume is increasing such that $\frac{dV}{dt} = 60\pi$ ft^3 / min. At that instant, what is the rate of change of the circumference of the snowball, in feet per minute?

(A) 10π
(B) $2\sqrt{3}\pi$
(C) 2π
(D) $\sqrt{3}\pi$
(E) π

15. For a right triangle with a base and a height of b and h, the area of the triangle is increasing. The area increases at a rate 6 times as fast as the height, and the base increases at a rate twice as fast as the height. When the base and height are equal, what are their lengths equal to?

(A) 8
(B) 4
(C) 2
(D) 1
(E) 0.5

16. A factory produces plastic toys in the shape of a cone, the volume of which is given by the formula $V = \frac{1}{3}\pi r^2 h$. After being made, the cones slowly cool and change size; the radius shrinks by $0.5 cm / hr$, and the height grows by $5 cm / hr$. When the radius of

the cone is *1cm* and the height of the cone is *4cm*, how is the volume of the cone changing?

(A) Increases at $1\pi cm^3 / hr$

(B) Decreases at $1 cm^3 / hr$

(C) Increases at $\pi cm^3 / hr$

(D) Decreases at $\pi cm^3 / hr$

(E) Increases at $3\pi cm^3 / hr$

17. A 13-foot ladder is leaning up against a wall. The floor is slick, so the bottom of the ladder slides away from the wall at a rate of 1 *ft*/ sec. When the bottom of the ladder is 5 feet away from the wall, what is the rate of change of the top of the ladder sliding down the wall?

(A) $\dfrac{5}{13}$ *ft*/ sec

(B) $-\dfrac{5}{12}$ *ft*/ sec

(C) $\dfrac{5}{6}$ *ft*/ sec

(D) $-\dfrac{5}{6}$ *ft*/ sec

(E) $\dfrac{12}{5}$ *ft*/ sec

18. A kiddie pool in the shape of a right cylinder is being drained of water for the winter. The volume of a cylinder is given by $V = \pi r^2 h$. The height of the water is dropping at a rate of $1\ ft/hr$. When full, the radius of the pool is $6\ ft$ and the height is $3\ ft$. The volume of water is decreasing by

(A) $6\pi\ ft^3$ per hr
(B) $12\pi\ ft^3$ per hr
(C) $36\pi\ ft^3$ per hr
(D) $72\ ft^3$ per hr
(E) $108\pi\ ft^3$ per hr

19. The function f is differentiable for all real numbers. The table below given values of the function and its derivative, $f'(x)$. If $f^{-1}(x)$ is the inverse of f, what is the slope of the normal line to the tangent at $f^{-1}(2)$?

x	f(x)	f'(x)
-3	2	4
2	-5	7

(A) $\dfrac{1}{4}$
(B) -4
(C) $\dfrac{1}{7}$
(D) -7
(E) $\dfrac{1}{7}$

20. The graph shown below is of $y = f^{-1}(x)$, which is the inverse of a differentiable function, f. The tangent to f^{-1} at the point (1, 5) is also shown. What is the equation of the tangent line to $f(x)$ at $x = 5$?

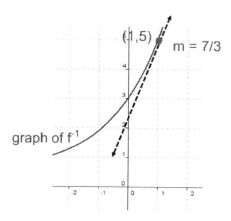

(A) $y - 1 = \dfrac{3}{7}(x - 5)$

(B) $y - 1 = -\dfrac{3}{7}(x - 5)$

(C) $y - 1 = \dfrac{7}{3}(x - 5)$

(D) $y - 5 = \dfrac{3}{7}(x - 1)$

(E) $y - 5 = -\dfrac{3}{7}(x - 1)$

21. A particle moves along the x-axis such that its position at time t is given by the equation $x(t) = \dfrac{t^3}{2} - t^2 + 9$. The acceleration of the particle at $t = 3$ is

    (A) 13.5
    (B) 11
    (C) 9
    (D) 7.5
    (E) 7

22. The velocity of a train travelling between two stations is given by $v(t) = 6t^2 - 4t + \dfrac{9}{2}$, where t is time. When the acceleration of the train is 2, its velocity is

    (A) 0
    (B) 0.5
    (C) 4
    (D) 6
    (E) 12.5

23. A particle moves along the x-axis such that its position at time t is given by the equation $x(t) = t^3 - 7.5t^2 + 18t$. During which intervals is the particle's velocity negative and acceleration positive?

    (A) $(2.5, 3)$
    (B) $(0, 2)$ and $(3, \infty)$
    (C) $(2, 2.5)$
    (D) $(2, 3)$
    (E) The particle never has a negative velocity and positive acceleration

24. A moving particle's velocity is given by the equation $v(t) = 2t^3 - 12t^2 + 10t$. At what time does the particle reach its absolute maximum acceleration on the interval $1 \leq t \leq 4$?

(A) -14
(B) 1
(C) 2
(D) 4
(E) 10

25. The velocity and acceleration of an amusement park ride, which moves horizontally, are shown below on the table below. The velocity and acceleration are both continuous and differentiable for all real numbers, and there are no other zeroes besides the ones included on the table. Which of the following statements are true?

t	0	1	2	3	4	5	6	7	8
v(t)	10	15	13	0	-5	-7	-2	0	2
a(t)	2	0	-3	-3	-1	0	5	2	0

(A) The ride is speeding up at $t = 2$
(B) The ride is moving right at $t = 4$
(C) The ride is speeding up at $t = 4$
(D) The ride is not moving at $t = 5$
(E) The ride is speeding up at $t = 8$

26. The position of a particle is shown below. Which of the following graphs below could be the graph of the velocity of the particle?

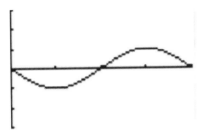

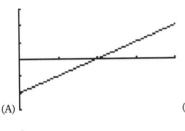
(A)

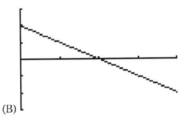
(B)

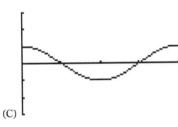
(C)

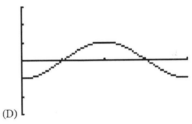
(D)

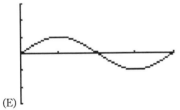
(E)

27. Along a number line, a particle is moving for a period of time from $0 < t < 8$. At $t = 0$, the particle begins at $x = 0$. At what time has the particle moved the farthest to the left?

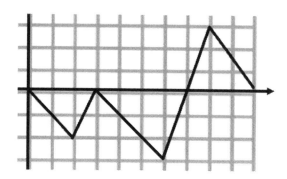

(A) 3
(B) 6
(C) 7
(D) 8
(E) 10

DIFFICULTY LEVEL 3

28. In a given rectangle, the two sides are each changing over time. The sides of the rectangle are named a and b. If there is an instant in time where the area of the rectangle is not changing, which of the equations below must be true at that instant?

(A) $a = b$

(B) $\dfrac{da}{dt} = \dfrac{db}{dt}$

(C) $\dfrac{da}{dt} = -\dfrac{db}{dt}$

(D) $a\dfrac{da}{dt} = b\dfrac{db}{dt}$

(E) $b\dfrac{da}{dt} = -a\dfrac{db}{dt}$

29. Train A leaves the station heading east at a rate of $15\,km/hr$. Train B leaves the station heading south at a rate of $10\,km/hr$. Let x be the distance between Train A and the station, let y be the distance between Train B and the station, and let θ be the angle, with its vertex at A, formed between the station and Train Find the rate of change of θ, in radians per hour, when $x = 3$ km and $y = 4$ km.

(A) $\dfrac{3}{2} rad/hr$

(B) $-\dfrac{2}{3} rad/hr$

(C) $\dfrac{18}{5} rad/hr$

(D) $-\dfrac{5}{6} rad/hr$

(E) $-\dfrac{6}{5} rad/hr$

30. The position of a particle moving along a line is given by $p(t) = 3\sin t - 2t + \pi$, where $0 \le t \le 2\pi$ is time. If, for some c such that $0 \le c \le 2\pi$, $v(c) = -2$ and $|a(c)| = 3$, then $p(c) =$

(A) π only
(B) 3 only
(C) π or 3
(D) $-3 - 2\pi$ only
(E) $-3 - 2\pi$ or 3

31. A position of an insect moving along a linear path at time t is given by the equation $x(t) = t^4 + 4t^3 + 15$. The insect is watched from [0,10] seconds. How many times in the interval [0, 10] are the insect's velocity and acceleration the same?

(A) Never
(B) 1
(C) 2
(D) 3
(E) 4

32. A particle moves along the x-axis in such a way that its position at time t ($t>0$) is $p(t) = \ln(t^3) + \dfrac{t^2}{2}$. At what time does the particle reach its minimum velocity?

(A) $\dfrac{\sqrt{3}}{3}$

(B) 1

(C) $e-1$

(D) $\sqrt{3}$

(E) 3

33. For an object moving with a velocity given by $v(t) = \dfrac{4t^3}{3} - 8t^2 + 12t + 2$, what is the difference between the object's maximum and minimum acceleration over the interval $0 \le t \le 3$?

(A) 22

(B) 16

(C) 12

(D) 4

(E) 2

34. A cart on a linear track has its position given at time t by the equation $x(t) = 12 + 26t - t^2$. The cart is begins moving at $t = 0$, and stops at $t = 5$. On which intervals is the speed of the cart increasing?

(A) $0 < t < 2.5$

(B) $2.5 < t < 5$

(C) $1 < t < 3$

(D) The speed of the cart is always increasing

(E) The speed of the cart is never increasing

35. The equation $x(t) = 12 + 26t - t^2$ given the position of a particle on the x-axis at time t on the interval $0 < t < 10$. The particle has a decrease in speed when

(A) $0 < t < 5$
(B) $2 < t < 8$
(C) $0 < t < 2$ and $5 < t < 8$
(D) $2 < t < 5$ only
(E) $2 < t < 5$ and $8 < t < 10$

COMPUTATION OF DERIVATIVES

PART 1

DIFFICULTY LEVEL 1

1. $\dfrac{d}{dx}\left(3x+\dfrac{1}{x}-\dfrac{1}{x^2}\right)$ when x = -1 is

   (A) 4
   (B) $\dfrac{7}{2}$
   (C) $\dfrac{19}{6}$
   (D) 2
   (E) $\dfrac{1}{6}$

2. For the function $g(x)=e^{\ln x^2}$, $g'(x)=$

   (A) $\dfrac{\ln x^2}{x}$
   (B) $2x^3$
   (C) $2x$
   (D) $\dfrac{1}{e^{x^2}}$
   (E) $\dfrac{1}{e^{2x}}$

3. $\dfrac{d}{dx}(3^x)$ when $x = 2$ is

 (A) 3
 (B) 6
 (C) $9\ln 3$
 (D) $3\ln 3$
 (E) $\dfrac{9}{\ln 3}$

4. If $f(x) = 2\sin x + \tan x$, then $f'(x)$ is

 (A) $2\cos x + \cot x$
 (B) $-2\cos x + \cot x$
 (C) $2\cos x - \cot x$
 (D) $-2\cos x + \sec^2 x$
 (E) $2\cos x + \sec^2 x$

DIFFICULTY LEVEL 2

5. Find $f'(x)$ when $f(x) = x^3 \ln x$.

 (A) $3x^2 \ln x$
 (B) $x^2(3\ln x + x)$
 (C) $x^2(3\ln x + 1)$
 (D) $3x$
 (E) $3x(x\ln x + 1)$

6. Which of the following represents $h'(x)$, if $h(x) = 2x\sqrt{3-x}$

   (A) $\dfrac{1}{\sqrt{3-x}}$

   (B) $\dfrac{2+x}{\sqrt{3-x}}$

   (C) $\dfrac{6}{\sqrt{3-x}}$

   (D) $\dfrac{6-3x}{\sqrt{3-x}}$

   (E) $\dfrac{6-x}{\sqrt{3-x}}$

7. If $f(x) = (x^2 - 3)^{\frac{1}{3}}$, then $f'(2)$ is

   (A) $-\dfrac{1}{3}$

   (B) 0

   (C) $\dfrac{1}{3}$

   (D) 1

   (E) $\dfrac{4}{3}$

8. The slope of the tangent line to the graph of $f(x) = (\ln x)^2$ when $x = e$ is

   (A) $\dfrac{1}{e}$

   (B) $\dfrac{2}{e}$

   (C) 0

   (D) 1

   (E) 2

9. What is the equation of the derivative of $g(x) = \dfrac{x^2}{3x-1}$?

(A) $\dfrac{3x^2-2x}{x^3}$

(B) $\dfrac{2x-3x^2}{x^3}$

(C) $\dfrac{2x-3x^2}{(3x-1)^2}$

(D) $\dfrac{3x^2-2x}{(3x-1)^2}$

(E) $\dfrac{9x^2-2x}{(3x-1)^2}$

10. The instantaneous rate of change at x = -1 of the function $f(x) = \dfrac{3x}{2x-2}$ is

   (A) $-\dfrac{9}{8}$

   (B) $-\dfrac{3}{8}$

   (C) $\dfrac{-3}{2}$

   (D) $\dfrac{3}{8}$

   (E) Does not exist

11. If $f(x) = \cos x(\sec x + \tan x)$, then $f'(x)$ is

   (A) $\sin x(\csc x + \cot x)$
   (B) $-\sin x\sec x(\tan x+1)(\tan x+\sec x)$
   (C) $-\sin x\sec x(\tan x+\sec x)$
   (D) $\cos x$
   (E) $\sec^2 x$

12. If $y = \dfrac{2x}{\ln x}$, then $\dfrac{dy}{dx} =$

   (A) $2x$

   (B) $\dfrac{2}{x}$

(C) $\dfrac{1}{\ln x}$

(D) $\dfrac{2(\ln x - 1)}{(\ln x)^2}$

(E) $-\dfrac{2(\ln x - 1)}{(\ln x)^2}$

13. What is the slope of the tangent line at x = 0 of $f(x) = 2^x (\cos x)$?

    (A) $\ln 2$
    (B) $1 + \ln 2$
    (C) 2
    (D) 1
    (E) 0

14. If $y = 3 \sin 2x$, then $\dfrac{d^2 y}{dx^2} =$

    (A) $12 x^2 \sin 2x$
    (B) $6 \sin 2x$
    (C) $6 \cos 2x$
    (D) $-3 \sin 2x$
    (E) $-12 \sin 2x$

15. If $f(x) = (2x-1)^3$, then the third derivative of $f(x)$ at $x = 0$ is

 (A) 48
 (B) 24
 (C) 2
 (D) 0
 (E) -1

16. What is the instant rate of change of $f(x) = (3x+2)(x-3)^2$ when $x = 2$?

 (A) -16
 (B) -13
 (C) -5
 (D) 5
 (E) 8

17. For the function $g(x) = \ln(\dfrac{e}{x^2 - 5x})$, $g'(x) =$

 (A) $\dfrac{x^2 - 5x}{e}$
 (B) $x^2 - 5x$
 (C) $\dfrac{2x-5}{e(x^2 - 5x)}$
 (D) $\dfrac{5 - 2x}{x^2 - 5x}$
 (E) $\dfrac{2x - 5}{x^2 - 5x}$

18. Two differentiable functions, f and g, are given such that $f(g(x)) = \dfrac{1}{x}$. If $f'(4) = 2$ and $g(0.5) = 4$, then $g'(0.5) =$

   (A) 4
   (B) 1
   (C) -0.5
   (D) -2
   (E) -4

19. If $y = u^2$ and $u = \tan x$, then what is $\dfrac{dy}{dx}$ at $x = \dfrac{\pi}{3}$?

   (A) $\dfrac{\pi^2}{9}$
   (B) $\sqrt{3}$
   (C) 3
   (D) 8
   (E) $8\sqrt{3}$

20. For the function $f(x) = \arctan(3x)$, $f'(x) =$

   (A) $\dfrac{3}{1+9x^2}$
   (B) $\dfrac{1}{1+9x^2}$
   (C) $\dfrac{1}{1+3x^2}$
   (D) $\operatorname{arcsec}^2(3x)$
   (E) $3\operatorname{arcsec}^2(3x)$

DIFFICULTY LEVEL 3

21. $\dfrac{d}{dx}\left(\cos^2(3x)\right)$ is

(A) $-6\sin(3x)\cos(3x)$
(B) $6\cos(3x)$
(C) $-2\sin(3x)\cos(3x)$
(D) $-3\sin^2(3x)$
(E) $-6\sin(3x)$

22. $\dfrac{d}{dx}\left(-\cos(e^{-x})\right)$ at x = 1 is

(A) $\dfrac{\sin(e)}{e}$

(B) $\dfrac{\sin(\frac{1}{e})}{e}$

(C) $-\dfrac{\sin(\frac{1}{e})}{e}$

(D) $\dfrac{\sin(-e)}{e}$

(E) $-e(\sin(-e))$

23. The differentiable function f is defined such that $f(x) = \dfrac{g(x)}{1+x^2}$, where g is another differentiable function. If $f'(-1) = 5$ and $g'(-1) = 3$, then $g(-1) =$

(A) 2
(B) 5
(C) 7
(D) 17
(E) Not enough information to find $g(-1)$

24. $\dfrac{d}{dx}\left(\sqrt[3]{\sin(\pi x)}\right)$ is

(A) $\dfrac{\pi}{3\sqrt[3]{\cos^2(\pi x)}}$

(B) $\dfrac{\pi}{3\sqrt[3]{\sin^2(\pi x)}}$

(C) $\dfrac{\pi \cos(\pi x)}{3\sqrt[3]{\sin^2(\pi x)}}$

(D) $\dfrac{2\pi \cos(\pi x)}{3\sqrt[3]{\sin^2(\pi x)}}$

(E) $-\dfrac{\pi}{3\sqrt[3]{\cos^2(\pi x)}}$

25. The differentiable function f is defined such that $f(x) = \dfrac{(g(x))^2}{2h(x)}$, where g and h are both differentiable functions as well. Values for g and h are given in the table below. If $f'(2) = -4$, find k.

x	g(x)	g'(x)	h(x)	h'(x)
2	1	-3	2	k

(A) -44

(B) -22

(C) 44

(D) 20

(E) 14

26. What is the equation of the tangent line to the function $f(x) = \arcsin(2x)$ at $x = \dfrac{1}{4}$?

(A) $y - \dfrac{\pi}{6} = \sqrt{3}(x - \dfrac{1}{4})$

(B) $y - \dfrac{1}{2} = \dfrac{4\sqrt{3}}{3}(x - \dfrac{1}{4})$

(C) $y - \dfrac{\pi}{6} = \dfrac{4\sqrt{3}}{3}(x - \dfrac{1}{4})$

(D) $y - \dfrac{1}{2} = \sqrt{3}(x - \dfrac{1}{4})$

(E) $y - \dfrac{2\pi}{3} = \dfrac{4\sqrt{3}}{3}(x - \dfrac{1}{4})$

27. The function $g(x) = \sin(\arccos x)$ has a derivative given by

(A) $(\cos x)(\dfrac{-1}{\sqrt{1-x^2}} + \arccos x)$

(B) $\dfrac{x}{1-x}$

(C) $\dfrac{1}{1-x}$

(D) $-\dfrac{x}{\sqrt{1-x^2}}$

(E) $-\dfrac{1}{\sqrt{1-x^2}}$

Computation of Derivatives

PART 2

DIFFICULTY LEVEL 1

1. If $xy - x^3 = 5$, then find $\dfrac{dy}{dx}$ at the point (-1, -4).

   (A) –12
   (B) –7
   (C) –1
   (D) 1
   (E) 3

2. In the figure below, the slope field comes from which differential equation?

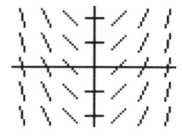

   (A) $\dfrac{dy}{dx} = y$

   (B) $\dfrac{dy}{dx} = x$

   (C) $\dfrac{dy}{dx} = x + y$

   (D) $\dfrac{dy}{dx} = xy$

   (E) $\dfrac{dy}{dx} = x^2$

3. For the given slope field, the differential equation that generated it is

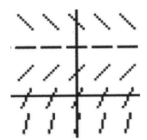

(A) $\dfrac{dy}{dx} = y+2$

(B) $\dfrac{dy}{dx} = y-2$

(C) $\dfrac{dy}{dx} = 2-y$

(D) $\dfrac{dy}{dx} = 2y$

(E) $\dfrac{dy}{dx} = \dfrac{1}{y-2}$

4. Which differential equation could have produced the slope field below?

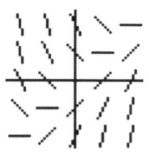

(A) $\dfrac{dy}{dx} = y$

(B) $\dfrac{dy}{dx} = x$

(C) $\dfrac{dy}{dx} = x + y$

(D) $\dfrac{dy}{dx} = y - x$

(E) $\dfrac{dy}{dx} = x - y$

5. Which differential equation created the given slope field?

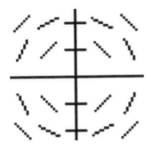

(A) $\dfrac{dy}{dx} = -\dfrac{x}{y}$

(B) $\dfrac{dy}{dx} = \dfrac{x}{y}$

(C) $\dfrac{dy}{dx} = \dfrac{-y}{x}$

(D) $\dfrac{dy}{dx} = x^2 + y^2$

(E) $\dfrac{dy}{dx} = 2x$

DIFFICULTY LEVEL 2

6. Find the slope of the tangent line to the curve $3xy - y^2 = 2x$ at $(1, 2)$

   (A) $-\dfrac{2}{3}$

   (B) $-\dfrac{1}{4}$

   (C) 2

   (D) $\dfrac{9}{4}$

   (E) 4

7. If $x^2 + xy - 4y^2 = 10$, then $\dfrac{dy}{dx}$ is

   (A) $\dfrac{-2x}{1-8y}$

   (B) $\dfrac{-2x}{x-8y}$

   (C) $-\dfrac{2x+y}{x-8}$

   (D) $\dfrac{2x+y}{x-8y}$

   (E) $-\dfrac{2x+y}{x-8y}$

8. Find $\dfrac{dy}{dx}$ when y = 1 on the curve given by $2xy - y^2 = 9$

    (A) $-\dfrac{1}{5}$

    (B) $-\dfrac{1}{4}$

    (C) 2

    (D) $\dfrac{3}{4}$

    (E) Not enough information to find $\dfrac{dy}{dx}$

9. At x = 2, find the slope of the tangent line to the curve $xy^2 + 6y = 10x$ in the first quadrant.

    (A) $-\dfrac{14}{15}$

    (B) $\dfrac{15}{14}$

    (C) $\dfrac{3}{7}$

    (D) $\dfrac{5}{7}$

    (E) $\dfrac{9}{2}$

10. What is the slope of the line tangent to the curve of $x^2 \ln y = y$ at the point $\left(\sqrt{e}, e\right)$?

    (A) 0

    (B) $2e^{\frac{3}{2}}$

    (C) $\dfrac{2}{e^{\frac{3}{2}}}$

    (D) $-\dfrac{2}{e^{\frac{3}{2}}}$

    (E) No slope

11. The equation of the tangent line to $y^2 + x^2 = 2y+12$ at (3, 1) is

   (A) $y+1 = \frac{1}{2}(x-3)$

   (B) $y+1 = 2(x-3)$

   (C) $y+1 = \frac{3}{2}(x-3)$

   (D) $y+1 = -\frac{3}{2}(x-3)$

   (E) $y+1 = -\frac{5}{2}(x-3)$

12. If $\dfrac{dy}{dx} = \dfrac{-y}{4y+x}$, find the value of the $\dfrac{d^2y}{dx^2}$ at (-2, 1).

   (A) 0

   (B) $-\dfrac{1}{2}$

   (C) $-\dfrac{1}{4}$

   (D) $\dfrac{1}{2}$

   (E) $\dfrac{1}{4}$

13. The behavior of the curve defined by $y^2 - 2x^3 - 11 = 0$ at (-1, 3) is

   (A) Increasing and concave up
   (B) Decreasing and concave up
   (C) Increasing and concave down
   (D) Decreasing and concave down
   (E) Horizontal slope and concave up

14. The slope field for a certain differential equation is shown below. Which of the following could be a specific solution to the differential equation?

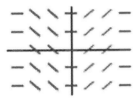

(A) $y = e^x$
(B) $y = e^{-x}$
(C) $y = \sin x$
(D) $y = \cos x$
(E) $y = -\cos x$

15. The slope field for a certain differential equation is shown below. Which of the following could be a specific solution to the differential equation?

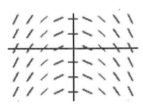

(A) $y = \dfrac{x}{2}$

(B) $y = -\dfrac{x}{2}$

(C) $y = \dfrac{x^2}{4}$

(D) $y = -\dfrac{x^2}{4}$

(E) $y = 2x$

16. Which slope field can be generated by the following differential equation: $\dfrac{dy}{dx} = 2x + y$

(A)

(B)

(C)

(D)

(E)

17. Which slope field can be generated by the following differential equation: $\dfrac{dy}{dx} = e^x$

(A)   (B)

(C)   (D)

(E)

DIFFICULTY LEVEL 3

18. Given the equation $\cos x = e^{2y}$, with $0 < x < \pi$, what is the derivative in terms of x?

    (A) $-\dfrac{\sin x}{2}$

    (B) $-\dfrac{\tan x}{2}$

    (C) $\sin x$

    (D) $\tan x$

    (E) $-\cot x$

19. The curve defined by $3xy + y^2 = -10x$ has a single horizontal tangent line. What is the equation of the normal to this horizontal tangent line?

    (A) $x = -6$
    (B) $x = -4$
    (C) $x = 0$
    (D) $x = 8$
    (E) $x = \dfrac{40}{9}$

20. For the equation of the curve given by $2x^2 + y^2 = 9$, $\dfrac{d^2 y}{dx^2}$ at the point (2, -1) is

    (A) 0
    (B) 4
    (C) 6
    (D) 18
    (E) Undefined

21. If $x^2 + y^2 = 36$, what is $\dfrac{d^2 y}{dx^2}$?

(A) $\dfrac{1}{36}$

(B) $\dfrac{-36}{y^3}$

(C) $\dfrac{-1}{y^2}$

(D) $\dfrac{x^2 - y^2}{y^3}$

(E) $\dfrac{x + y}{y^2}$

THE FOUR THEOREMS (EXTRA)

DIFFICULTY LEVEL 1

1. If $f(x) = \begin{cases} x^2 + 2, & -3 \le x < -1 \\ 3x+5, & -1 \le x \le 3 \end{cases}$, then why does the graph of f fail to have a minimum value on the interval [-3, 3]?

    (A) f is not continuous at x = -1
    (B) f is not differentiable at x = -1
    (C) Graphs of functions are guaranteed a minimum or maximum value, but not both
    (D) Piecewise functions never have minimums or maximums
    (E) There is a minimum at (-1, 1)

2. The function g is continuous on the interval [-6, -4], and has values given by the table below. It is known that the equation $g(x) = \dfrac{-3}{4}$ has at least two solutions in the given interval if a is

x	-6	-5	-4
g(x)	2	a	1

    (A) 0
    (B) $\dfrac{3}{2}$
    (C) $-\dfrac{3}{4}$
    (D) -4
    (E) 2

3. The function f is continuous on the interval [-1, 4] and has values given by $f(-1) = 2$, $f(2) = k$, and $f(4) = 0$. If $f(x) = 7$ at least twice in the interval [-1, 4] for some x, then must k be
    (A) -8
    (B) 0

(C) 3
(D) 7
(E) 9

4. For a function f that is continuous and not a linear equation for $-1 \leq x \leq 5$. f has function values given by $f(-1) = 3$, and $f(5) = 3$. If there are no values of c such that $f'(c) = 0$ for $-1 \leq c \leq 5$, which statement must be true?

   (A) For all c, $-1 \leq c \leq 5$, $f'(c) < 0$
   (B) For all c, $-1 \leq c \leq 5$, $f'(c) > 0$
   (C) For some c, $-1 \leq c \leq 5$, $f'(c)$ does not exist
   (D) $f(-1)$ and $f(3)$ should be equal to 0
   (E) f cannot be a continuous function

DIFFICULTY LEVEL 2

5. Let f be a continuous function on the interval $[1, 9]$. If $f(1) = 5$, $f(3) = -2$, and $f(9) = 6$, then which of the following statements are true?

   I. f has at least 2 zeroes
   II. For some c, $1 \leq c \leq 9$, $f(c) \leq f(x)$
   III. For some c, $1 < c < 9$, $f(c) = 8$

   (A) I only
   (B) III only
   (C) I and II only
   (D) I and III only
   (E) All are true

6. The Mean Value Theorem states that a certain point must exist on the graph of $f(x) = 2x^2 - 6x + 5$ on the interval $[-1, 3]$. This point is

   (A) $(1, -2)$
   (B) $(1, 1)$
   (C) $(-1, -10)$

(D) $(-1, 13)$

(E) $(-2, 25)$

7. For the function $f(x) = e^{2x}$, there exists a number, c, on the interval of $[0, 2]$ that satisfies the conclusion of the Mean Value Theorem. This number is

(A) $\frac{1}{2}\ln(\frac{e^4-1}{4})$

(B) $\frac{1}{2}\ln(\frac{e^4-1}{8})$

(C) $\ln(\frac{e^4-1}{16})$

(D) $\ln(\frac{e^4-1}{4})$

(E) $\ln(\frac{e^4}{16})$

8. The Mean Value Theorem states that a certain value, c, must exist on the graph of $f(x) = x^3 + 2x^2$ on the interval $[-2, 0]$. What are all possible values for c?

(A) 0 and -1

(B) -1 and $\frac{-4}{3}$

(C) 0 only

(D) -1 only

(E) $\frac{-4}{3}$ only

9. The graph of a continuous function, g, is shown below on the interval $[-8, 6]$. The graph consists of a smooth curve and a line. If we restrict the domain using a value, k, from $[-8, k]$ where the Mean Value Theorem would apply and guarantee that $g'(c) = \frac{1}{2}$ for some c in the interval. What are the possible values of k?

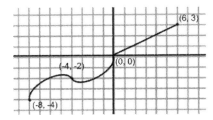

(A) -4 only
(B) 0 only
(C) 6 only
(D) -4 and 0 only
(E) -4, 0 and 6

10. The function f is differentiable on the interval [3, 9], and has values given by the table below. Which of the following statements must be true?

x	3	4	6	8	9
f(x)	20	15	7	12	18

I. The minimum value of f on [3, 9] is 7
II. For some c, $3 \le c \le 9$, $f'(c) = 0$
III. $f(x) = 10$ at least twice on [3, 9]

(A) I only
(B) II only
(C) III only
(D) I and III only
(E) II and III only

11. For the function f that is continuous and differentiable on the interval [0, 5], which of the following is false?

(A) For some c in [0, 5], $f'(c) = 0$
(B) For some c in [0, 5], $f'(c)$ does not exist
(C) For some c in [0, 5], $f(c)$ is a minimum
(D) For some c in [0, 5], $f(c)$ is a maximum
(E) For some c in [0, 5], $f'(c) = \dfrac{f(b) - f(a)}{b-a}$

DIFFICULTY LEVEL 3

12. A highway is monitored for traffic during a 6-hour period. The amount of cars on the highway is modeled by the differentiable function $h(t)$ where t is measured in hours. For $0 \le t \le 6$, what is the fewest number of times that $h'(t) = 0$?

t	0	1	2	3	4	5	6
h(t)	50	65	40	25	25	35	10

(A) 0
(B) 1
(C) 2
(D) 3
(E) 4

13. For the function f that is continuous and differentiable on the interval $[-3, 1]$, and $f(-3) = 7$, and $f(1) = k$. which of the following are true?

I. If $k = 0$, then for some c, $-3 \le c \le 1$, $f(c) = 3.5$
II. If $k = 7$, then for some c, $-3 \le c \le 1$, $f'(c) = 0$
III. If $k = 15$, then for some c, $-3 \le c \le 1$, $f'(c) = 2$

(A) II only
(B) I and II only
(C) I and III only
(D) II and III only
(E) All statements are true

INTERPRETATIONS AND PROPERTIES OF DEFINITE INTEGRALS

DIFFICULTY LEVEL 1

1. $\int_{1}^{2}(6x^2-5)\,dx=$

    (A) 36
    (B) 12
    (C) 9
    (D) 6
    (E) 3

2. $\int_{1}^{2}\dfrac{2}{x^3}\,dx=$

    (A) $\dfrac{3}{4}$
    (B) $-\dfrac{5}{4}$
    (C) -7
    (D) $\dfrac{15}{32}$
    (E) $\dfrac{45}{8}$

3. A particle moves along a horizontal axis such that its velocity is given by $v(t) = 6t-4$. What is the displacement of the particle between the times $t=2$ and $t=3$?

   (A) 41
   (B) 33
   (C) 26
   (D) 19
   (E) 11

4. The graph of f, a differentiable function, is even. If $\int_0^{-1} f(x)\,dx = 3$, then $\int_{-1}^{1} f(x)\,dx =$

   (A) -6
   (B) -3
   (C) 0
   (D) 3
   (E) 6

5. $\int_0^x -2\sin t\,dt =$

   (A) $-2\sin x$
   (B) $2\cos x$
   (C) $-2\cos x$
   (D) $2\cos x - 2$
   (E) $2 - 2\cos x$

6. $\dfrac{d}{dx}\displaystyle\int_0^x \ln(t^2+2)\,dt =$

   (A) $\dfrac{1}{x^2+2}$

   (B) $\dfrac{2x}{x^2+2}$

   (C) $\ln(x^2)$

   (D) $\ln(x^2+2)$

   (E) $2x\ln(x^2+2)$

DIFFICULTY LEVEL 2

7. $\displaystyle\int_{-1}^{0} (2x-1)^2\,dx =$

   (A) $-\dfrac{13}{3}$

   (B) $\dfrac{13}{3}$

   (C) -4

   (D) 4

   (E) 12

8. Find the area under the curve of $\dfrac{2x^2+1}{x}$ over the interval $[1,2]$.

   (A) $\ln 2$
   (B) 3
   (C) $3+\ln 2$
   (D) 4
   (E) $\dfrac{33}{4}$

9. For the integral $\displaystyle\int_{-2}^{a} x\,dx = 0$, what values of a satisfy the equation?

(A) −2
(B) 0
(C) 2
(D) −2 and 2
(E) −2, 0, and 2

10. If $\int_{\frac{\pi}{2}}^{\pi}(\cos t + k)\,dt = 3\pi - 1$, then $k =$

(A) $\dfrac{1}{2}$
(B) 1
(C) 2
(D) π
(E) 4

11. A differentiable function f exists over the interval $[1,3]$ such that $-1 \le f(x) \le 5$. What is the range of the possible values of $\int_{1}^{3} f(x)\,dx$?

(A) $[-2, 10]$
(B) $[-1, 5]$
(C) $[-1, 15]$
(D) $[1, 3]$
(E) $[1, 15]$

Interpretations and Properties of Definite Integrals

12. If $\int_1^k f(x)\,dx = 2k-3$, then $\int_1^k (f(x)+3)\,dx =$

    (A) $2k-4$
    (B) $2k$
    (C) $5k-6$
    (D) $5k-4$
    (E) $5k$

13. $\int_2^{100} f(x)\,dx + \int_{100}^1 f(x)\,dx =$

    (A) $\int_1^2 f(x)\,dx$

    (B) $-\int_1^2 f(x)\,dx$

    (C) $\int_2^{100} f(x)\,dx$

    (D) $-\int_2^{100} f(x)\,dx$

    (E) $\int_1^{200} f(x)\,dx$

14. If $\int_0^5 g(x)\,dx = a+b$ and $\int_5^3 g(x)\,dx = -a+2b$, then $\int_0^3 g(x)\,dx =$

    (A) 2a - b
    (B) -2a + b
    (C) 2a
    (D) -b
    (E) 3b

112

15. $\int_0^x t e^{t^2} dt =$

   (A) $2\left(e^{x^2} - 1\right)$

   (B) $\dfrac{1}{2} e^{x^2}$

   (C) $\dfrac{1}{2}\left(e^{x^2} - 1\right)$

   (D) $\dfrac{1}{2} x^2 e^{x^2}$

   (E) $\dfrac{1}{4} x^2 e^{x^2}$

16. $\dfrac{d}{dx} \int_x^2 \dfrac{2}{1-t^2} dt =$

   (A) $-\dfrac{2}{1-x^2}$

   (B) $\dfrac{2}{1-x^2}$

   (C) $-\dfrac{2}{3} - \dfrac{2}{1-x^2}$

   (D) $\dfrac{2}{3} + \dfrac{2}{1-x^2}$

   (E) $\dfrac{-4t}{(1-t^2)^2}$

17. If $F(x) = \int_0^x \frac{2}{1+t^3} dt$, then $F'(2) =$

(A) $-\frac{8}{27}$

(B) $-\frac{2}{9}$

(C) $\frac{2}{9}$

(D) $\frac{8}{27}$

(E) 2

18. Let f be the function given by $f(x) = \int_0^x (t-1)e^{t^2} dt$ for $-1 \le x \le 2$. When is f increasing?

(A) $(-1,0)$
(B) $(0,1)$
(C) $(0,2)$
(D) $(-1,0)$ and $(1,2)$
(E) $(1,2)$

19. The graph of the piecewise linear function f, shown below, is defined for $-4 \le x \le 10$. Let g be the function defined by $g(x) = \int_{-2}^x f(t)dt$. Which of the following is true?

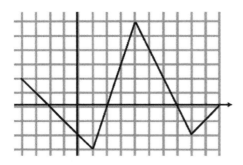

(A) $g(-4) < g(-2) < g(2) < g(7) < g(10)$

(B) $g(1) < g(8) < g(10) < g(-4) < g(4)$
(C) $g(2) < g(-4) < g(-2) < g(10) < g(7)$
(D) $g(4) < g(-4) < g(10) < g(8) < g(1)$
(E) $g(1) < g(-2) < g(2) < g(8) < g(4)$

DIFFICULTY LEVEL 3

20. A chemistry lab is heating a liquid solution, which increases in temperature at a rate of $2e^{2t}$ degrees per hour. When $t=0$, the temperature of the solution is $54°F$. What is the temperature of the solution when $t=4$, in degrees Fahrenheit?

(A) $e^8 + 53$
(B) $e^8 + 52$
(C) $e^8 - 1$
(D) $e^8 - 54$
(E) $e^8 - 55$

21. $\dfrac{d}{dx}\displaystyle\int_0^{x^2} \cos(t^3+1)\,dt =$

(A) $-\sin(x^6+1)$
(B) $\cos(x^3+1)$
(C) $\cos(x^6+1)$
(D) $2x\cos(x^6+1)$
(E) $6x^5\cos(x^6+1)$

22. The graph of the function f, shown below, is defined for $-3 \leq x \leq 7$. It has a horizontal tangent at x = 0. Let g be the continuous function defined by $g(x) = \displaystyle\int_0^x f(t)\,dt$. For what x-values does the graph of g have a point of inflection?

Interpretations and Properties of Definite Integrals

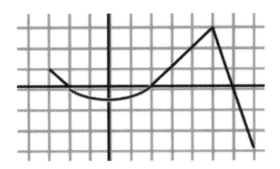

(A) 0 only
(B) 0 and 5
(C) 2 only
(D) -2, 2, and 6
(E) It has no points of inflection

APPLICATIONS OF INTEGRALS

DIFFICULTY LEVEL 1

1. The graph of a piece-wise linear function, f, is shown below for $-2 \leq x \leq 4$ for $t \geq 0$. What is the value of $\int_{-2}^{7} f(x)\,dx$?

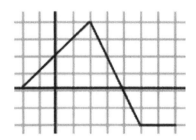

(A) 18
(B) 17
(C) 14
(D) 9
(E) 7

2. The area of the region enclosed by the graph of $y = x^2 + 3$ and $y = 7$ is

(A) $\dfrac{14}{3}$

(B) $\dfrac{16}{3}$

(C) $\dfrac{32}{3}$

(D) $\dfrac{104}{3}$

(E) 8π

3. The shaded area below is found using which expression?

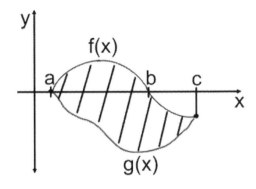

(A) $\displaystyle\int_a^b f(x)\,dx - \int_a^c g(x)\,dx$

(B) $\displaystyle\int_a^c (f(x) - g(x))\,dx$

(C) $\displaystyle\int_a^c (g(x) - f(x))\,dx$

(D) $\displaystyle\int_a^c (|f(x)| - |g(x)|)\,dx$

(E) $\displaystyle\int_a^b (f(x) - g(x))\,dx - \int_b^c (g(x) - f(x))\,dx$

4. The average value of $\sec^2 x$ on the interval $[2,5]$ is

   (A) $\dfrac{\tan 5 - \tan 2}{3}$

   (B) $\dfrac{\tan 5 - \tan 2}{7}$

   (C) $\dfrac{\tan 5 + \tan 2}{3}$

   (D) $\dfrac{\tan 5 + \tan 2}{7}$

   (E) $\dfrac{\tan 2 - \tan 5}{7}$

5. What is the average value of $6x^2 - x$ over the interval $-1 \leq x \leq 2$?

   (A) $\dfrac{33}{2}$

   (B) 11

   (C) $\dfrac{19}{2}$

   (D) $\dfrac{11}{2}$

   (E) $\dfrac{25}{6}$

Applications of Integrals

DIFFICULTY LEVEL 2

6. The area between the graphs of $y = 2x$ and $y = x^2 - 4x + 5$ is

   (A) $\dfrac{32}{3}$

   (B) $\dfrac{91}{3}$

   (C) $\dfrac{124}{3}$

   (D) $\dfrac{280}{3}$

   (E) 2π

7. The area of the region between the curves $y = \dfrac{1}{x}$, $x = 1$, $x = e$ and the x-axis is

   (A) $2 - \dfrac{2}{e^2}$

   (B) $\dfrac{1}{e} - 1$

   (C) 1

   (D) $\ln|e-1|$

   (E) e

8. The region enclosed by the x-axis, $x = 2$, and $y = x$ is rotated around the x-axis. What is the volume of the solid generated?

   (A) 8π

   (B) $\dfrac{8\pi}{3}$

   (C) 4π

   (D) $\dfrac{8\pi^2}{3}$

   (E) $4\pi^2$

9. The base of a solid is given by the function $y=\sqrt{x}$, bounded by the x-axis and $x=4$. The cross-sections of the solid are rectangles where the height is 5 times the measure of the width. The volume of this solid is

   (A) 40
   (B) 20
   (C) 10
   (D) 20π
   (E) 10π

10. The velocity of a particle moving horizontally is modeled by the function $v(t) = 2e^{\frac{t}{3}}$. Over the interval $1 \leq x \leq 3$, the particle's average velocity is

    (A) $6\left(e - \dfrac{1}{\sqrt[3]{e}}\right)$
    (B) $6(e - \sqrt[3]{e})$
    (C) $3e - \sqrt[3]{e}$
    (D) $3\left(e - \dfrac{1}{\sqrt[3]{e}}\right)$
    (E) $3(e - \sqrt[3]{e})$

DIFFICULTY LEVEL 3

11. The area of the region bound by graphs of $x = y^2$ and $x = 4$ is found using

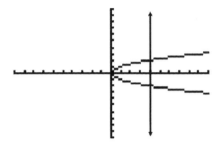

(A) $\int_0^4 (4 - \sqrt{x})\,dx$

(B) $\int_0^4 (\sqrt{x})\,dx$

(C) $\int_{-2}^2 (4 - y^2)\,dy$

(D) $\int_0^4 (4 - y^2)\,dy$

(E) $\int_{-2}^2 (y^2 - 4)\,dy$

12. The region, R, bounded by the x-axis, $y = \sqrt{x}$, and $x = 4$ is separated into two regions by the vertical line $x = k$. This divides R into two equal regions. The value of k is

(A)
(B) $2\sqrt{2}$
(C) $\sqrt[3]{16}$
(D) $\dfrac{3}{\sqrt{2}}$
(E) 2

13. The integral which would give the volume of the solid generated when the region bounded by $y = x^2 + 6$, $x = -1$, $x = 1$, and $y = 4$ is revolved around the line $y = 4$ is

(A) $\pi \int_{1}^{1} (x^2 + 6)^2 \, dx$

(B) $\pi \int_{1}^{1} ((x^2 + 6)^2 - (4)^2) \, dx$

(C) $\pi \int_{1}^{1} (x^2 + 2)^2 \, dx$

(D) $\int_{1}^{1} (x^2 + 6) \, dx$

(E) $\int_{1}^{1} (x^2 + 2) \, dx$

14. The volume of the solid generated when the shaded region bounded by $y=\dfrac{1}{x^2}$, $y=1$, and $x=4$ is revolved around the line $y=2$ is represented by

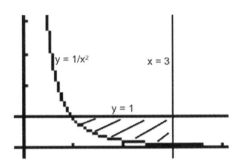

(A) $\pi\int_{1}^{3}((2-\dfrac{1}{x^2})^2 -(1)^2)\,dx$

(B) $\pi\int_{1}^{3}(2-\dfrac{1}{x^2})^2\,dx$

(C) $\pi\int_{1}^{3}(\dfrac{1}{x^2}-2)^2\,dx$

(D) $\pi\int_{1}^{3}((2)^2 -((\dfrac{1}{x^2}-1)^2)\,dx$

(E) $\pi\int_{1}^{3}(1-\dfrac{1}{x^2})^2\,dx$

15. The integral which would give the volume of the solid generated when the region bounded by the y-axis, $y=2x$, and $y=6$ is revolved around the y-axis is

   (A) $\pi \int_0^3 (2x)^2 \, dx$

   (B) $\pi \int_0^3 ((2x)^2 - (6)^2) \, dx$

   (C) $\pi \int_0^6 ((6)^2 - (\frac{y}{2})^2) \, dy$

   (D) $\pi \int_0^3 (\frac{y}{2})^2 \, dy$

   (E) $\pi \int_0^6 (\frac{y}{2})^2 \, dy$

16. The region enclosed by the x-axis, $y=\sqrt{x}$, and $x=4$ is rotated around the y-axis. What is the volume of the solid generated?

   (A) 4π
   (B) 8π
   (C) $\dfrac{44\pi}{3}$
   (D) $\dfrac{128\pi}{5}$
   (E) $\dfrac{88\pi}{3}$

17. The rate of change in the amount of people on line at the Rockin' Roller Coaster is given by $p(t) = 10\left(t^2 - 5t + 4\right)$ where $0 \le t \le 8$ is in hours and $p(t)$ is in people per hour. At the beginning of the day, there are 30 people already on line. Which expression below would give the number of people on line 3 hours after opening?

(A) $p(3)$

(B) $30 + p(3)$

(C) $\int_0^3 p(t)\,dt$

(D) $30 + \int_0^3 p(t)\,dt$

(E) $\int_0^3 p(t)\,dt - 30$

TECHNIQUES OF ANTIDIFFERENTIATION

DIFFICULTY LEVEL 1

1. $\int \sec x \tan x \, dx =$

   (A) $\sec x + C$
   (B) $\tan x + C$
   (C) $\sec x (\tan^2 x + \sec^2 x) + C$
   (D) $\ln |\sin x| + C$
   (E) $2\sin x \cos x + C$

2. $\int \dfrac{3}{\sqrt{1-x^2}} \, dx =$

   (A) $3x - 3\ln|x| + C$
   (B) $\dfrac{3x}{\sqrt{x - \dfrac{x^3}{3}}} + C$
   (C) $\dfrac{3x}{\sqrt{(1-x^2)^3}} + C$
   (D) $\arcsin x + C$
   (E) $3\ln(\sqrt{1-x^2}) + C$

3. $\int_0^{\frac{\pi}{6}} \cos(2x)\,dx =$

(A) $\dfrac{1}{4}$

(B) $\dfrac{1}{2}$

(C) $\sqrt{3}$

(D) $\dfrac{\sqrt{3}}{2}$

(E) $\dfrac{\sqrt{3}}{4}$

4. $\int_2^4 3e^{\frac{x}{4}}\,dx =$

(A) $\dfrac{1}{4}\left(e - \sqrt{e}\right)$

(B) $\dfrac{3}{4}\left(e - \sqrt{e}\right)$

(C) $\dfrac{12}{5}\left(e^5 - \sqrt{e^5}\right)$

(D) $3\left(e - \sqrt{e}\right)$

(E) $12\left(e - \sqrt{e}\right)$

Techniques of Antidifferentiation

5. If $U = 5x+6$, then the integral $\int_{-1}^{2} \sqrt{5x+6}\,dx$, when expressed in terms of U is equal to

   (A) $\int_{-1}^{2} U^{\frac{1}{2}}\,dU$

   (B) $\frac{1}{5}\int_{-1}^{2} U^{\frac{1}{2}}\,dU$

   (C) $\int_{1}^{16} U^{\frac{1}{2}}\,dU$

   (D) $\frac{1}{5}\int_{1}^{16} U^{\frac{1}{2}}\,dU$

   (E) $\int_{-1}^{4} U^{\frac{1}{2}}\,dU$

6. If $\int_{1}^{5} f(x+2)\,dx = 11$, then $\int_{3}^{7} f(x)\,dx =$

   (A) 9
   (B) 11
   (C) 13
   (D) −11
   (E) −13

DIFFICULTY LEVEL 2

7. $\int \dfrac{x\sec^2 x - 1}{x} dx =$

(A) $\tan x - \ln|x| + C$

(B) $\tan x + C$

(C) $\dfrac{x\tan x - 2}{x} + C$

(D) $2\sec^2 x\tan x + \dfrac{1}{x^2} + C$

(E) $\dfrac{\sec^3 x}{3} - \ln|x| + C$

8. $\int_{\pi/4}^{\pi/3} \dfrac{\sec^2 \theta}{\tan \theta} d\theta =$

(A) $\ln\dfrac{\pi}{3} - \ln\dfrac{\pi}{4}$

(B) $\ln\sqrt{3}$

(C) $\ln\sqrt{3} - 1$

(D) $\sqrt{3}$

(E) $\dfrac{\pi}{12}$

9. If $f'(x) = x^2 e^{x^3}$, then $f(x) =$

   (A) $\dfrac{1}{3} x^3 e^{x^3} + C$

   (B) $3 x^3 e^{x^3} + C$

   (C) $\dfrac{1}{3} e^{x^3} + C$

   (D) $3 e^{x^3} + C$

   (E) $\dfrac{e^{x^3}}{2x} + C$

10. $\displaystyle\int \dfrac{6x}{\sqrt{3-x^2}} dx =$

    (A) $-6\sqrt{3-x^2} + C$

    (B) $-3\sqrt{3-x^2} + C$

    (C) $\ln \sqrt{3-x^2} + C$

    (D) $\ln(3-x^2) + C$

    (E) $6x\ln\sqrt{3-x^2} + C$

DIFFICULTY LEVEL 3

11. If $\displaystyle\int_0^k \dfrac{e^{\sin x}}{\sec x} dx = \sqrt{e} - 1$, then $k =$

    (A) 0

    (B) $\dfrac{1}{2}$

    (C) 1

    (D) $\dfrac{\pi}{6}$

    (E) $\dfrac{\pi}{2}$

APPLICATIONS OF ANTIDIFFERENTIATION

DIFFICULTY LEVEL 1

1. A particle moves along the x-axis so that its velocity is modeled by $v(t) = -4t+15$ for $t \geq 0$. If the particle is at $x = -5$ when $t = 1$, where is the particle at $t = 3$?

   (A) 45
   (B) 33
   (C) 27
   (D) 22
   (E) 9

2. The acceleration of a particle is given by $a(t) = 2\sin t - 5$ for $t \geq 0$. Find the velocity of the particle at $t = \dfrac{\pi}{3}$, if its velocity at $t = 0$ is π?

   (A) $-1 - \dfrac{5\pi}{3}$
   (B) $1 - \dfrac{2\pi}{3}$
   (C) $3 - \dfrac{2\pi}{3}$
   (D) $3 + \dfrac{\pi}{3}$
   (E) π

DIFFICULTY LEVEL 2

3. The acceleration of a particle moving along horizontal line is $a(t) = 12t - 8$. If, when $t = 2$, the particle has a velocity of -1 and a position of 5, then the position $p(t) =$

   (A) $2t^3 - 4t^2 - 9t + 23$
   (B) $2t^3 - 4t^2 - 3t - 5$
   (C) $2t^3 - 4t^2$

(D) $6t^2 - 8t - 9$

(E) $24t^2 - 8t - 81$

4. An object has an acceleration given by $a(t) = 2 - 3t$. If the velocity of the object is -0.5 at $t=1$, and $p(t)$ is the position of the object relative to the origin at time t, what is $p(3) - p(1)$?

   (A) 15
   (B) 11
   (C) -5
   (D) -9
   (E) Not enough information to determine

5. A bug is walking along a fence so that its velocity is given by $v(t) = 4t - 12$. At $t = 4$, the bug's position is at -9, then the total distance the bug travels between $t = 0$ and $t = 4$ is

   (A) 20
   (B) 16
   (C) 10
   (D) -9
   (E) 2

6. A squirrel is climbing up a tree. The velocity of the squirrel, measured in inches per second, is given by the graph below. At $t=2$, the squirrel is 80 inches off of the ground. How many inches off of the ground is the squirrel at $t=7$?

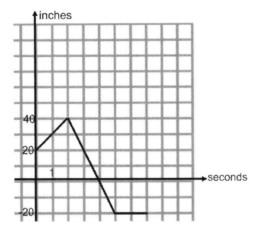

(A) 170
(B) 160
(C) 70
(D) 50
(E) 30

7. A particle is moving along a vertical axis, and its velocity, in inches per second, is given by the graph below. The particle starts 25 inches up on the axis. The total distance traveled in inches by the particle from 0 to 5 seconds is

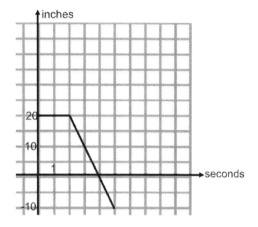

(A) 90
(B) 80
(C) 65
(D) 55
(E) 15

8. If $\frac{dy}{dx} = 6y$, and when $x = 0$, $y = 5$, then $y =$

(A) e^{6x}
(B) $5e^{6x}$
(C) $4 + e^{6x}$
(D) $5 + e^{6x}$
(E) $3x^2 + 5$

9. Given is the differential equation $\frac{dy}{dx} = 3y^2$. Find the slope of the curve of y when $x=0$, if when $x=1$, $y=\frac{1}{2}$.

   (A) 3
   (B) $\frac{3}{4}$
   (C) $\frac{3}{25}$
   (D) $\frac{3}{50}$
   (E) 0

10. $f'(x) = kf(x)$ where k is a non-zero constant. If $f(0) = 2$ and $f(1) = 2\sqrt{e}$, then $y=$

    (A) $e^{\frac{x}{2}}$
    (B) $2e^{-2x}$
    (C) $2e^{\frac{x}{2}}$
    (D) $1+2e^{\frac{x}{2}}$
    (E) $1+e^{\frac{x}{2}}$

DIFFICULTY LEVEL 3

11. If $\frac{dy}{dx} = \frac{3x^2}{y}$, and when $y=2$, $x=-1$, then when $y=16$, $x=$

    (A) 13
    (B) $\sqrt[3]{5}$
    (C) $\sqrt[3]{8}$
    (D) $\sqrt{8}$
    (E) $\sqrt{8198}$

12. The number of cells in a culture grows at a rate of $250e^{2t/3}$ per hour. When $t=0$, there are 400 cells in the culture. The numbers of cells in the culture when $t=3$ is

   (A) $\dfrac{500e^2}{3}$

   (B) $250e^2$

   (C) $250e^2 + 25$

   (D) $375e^2$

   (E) $375e^2 + 25$

13. The volume of water in a pool is being filled at a rate proportional to the square root of the volume. When $t=0$, the pool is empty, and at $t=8$, $V=4$. Which equation models the relationship between t and V?

   (A) $V = \dfrac{t}{2}$

   (B) $\sqrt{V} = 4t$

   (C) $\sqrt{V} = \dfrac{t}{4}$

   (D) $\sqrt{V^3} = 4t$

   (E) $\sqrt{V^3} = \dfrac{t}{4}$

NUMERICAL APPROXIMATIONS TO DEFINITE INTEGRALS

DIFFICULTY LEVEL 1

14. The function $f(x) = x^2 + 5$ is continuous on the interval [2, 8]. Using 3 equal subintervals, what is the Right Riemann approximation of $\int_2^8 f(x)\,dx$?

   (A) 142
   (B) 196
   (C) 197.5
   (D) 198
   (E) 262

15. For the graph of the function $y = f(x)$ shown below, the approximation of the area under the curve using a Left Riemann Sum with 3 subintervals of equal length is

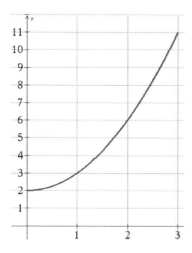

(A) 8
(B) 11
(C) 15.5
(D) 20
(E) 22

16. A table of values for a continuous function f is shown below. If three equal subintervals are used, which of the following is the midpoint approximation of $\int_0^6 f(x)\,dx$?

x	0	1	2	3	4	5	6
f(x)	12	8	16	20	20	14	10

(A) 84
(B) 94
(C) 120
(D) 138
(E) 143

17. The velocity of a train from 0 to 15 seconds is given in the table below, in feet per second. If the distance of the train at $t = 0$ is 12 feet from a point, what is the approximate distance at $t = 15$, using a Left Riemann Sum with 3 equal subintervals?

t	0	5	10	15
v(t)	3	7	5	2

(A) 75 feet
(B) 82 feet
(C) 87 feet
(D) 97 feet
(E) 127 feet

DIFFICULTY LEVEL 2

18. Approximate the value of $\int_{2}^{9} f(x)\,dx$ using the subintervals defined in the table below with the trapezoidal method.

x	2	4	5	9
f(x)	18	30	24	40

(A) 157
(B) 162
(C) 166
(D) 203
(E) 244

19. Below is the graph of the function $y = 64 - x^2$ where $0 \le x \le 8$. Using equal subintervals of length 2, the difference in the Left Riemann approximation and Right Riemann approximation is

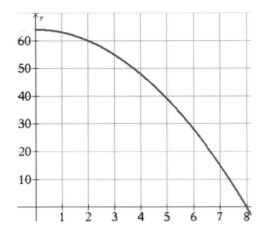

(A) 256
(B) 192
(C) 128
(D) 64
(E) There is no difference for this graph

20. The volume of water, in gallons per hour, that flowed through a river during a 16-hour period is shown below. Which of the following best approximates the total number of gallons of water that flowed through the river during those 16 hours?

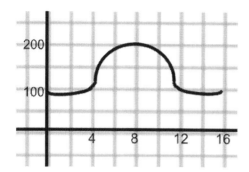

(A) 500
(B) 600
(C) 1600
(D) 2000
(E) 3200

21. The graph of the differentiable function $f(x)$ has the following properties over the interval [a, b]: $f'(x) > 0$ and $f''(x) > 0$. Which of the following Riemann Sums, using the same amount of sub-intervals, would be have to be an underestimate of $\int_a^b f(x)\,dx$?

(A) Left Riemann Sum
(B) Right Riemann Sum
(C) Midpoint Riemann Sum
(D) Trapezoidal Riemann Sum
(E) All are underestimates

DIFFICULTY LEVEL 3

22. The function $f(x) = 1 + \cos(\pi x)$ has a Riemann Sum approximation of 0, using two equal subintervals over the interval [0, 4]. Which Riemann Sum was used?

    (A) Left Riemann Sum
    (B) Right Riemann Sum
    (C) Midpoint Riemann Sum
    (D) Trapezoidal Riemann Sum
    (E) None of the methods has an approximation of 0

23. A Trapezoidal Riemann Sum was used to approximate $\int_1^2 f(x)\,dx$ using two subintervals defined in the table below. If the approximation is 18.5, the value of k is

x	1	k	2
f(x)	16	18	20

    (A) 1.2
    (B) 1.25
    (C) 1.5
    (D) 1.75
    (E) 1.8

24. The value of $\int_1^3 \frac{1}{x^2} dx$ is estimated using a Midpoint Riemann Sum of 2 equal subintervals. What is the difference between the exact value of $\int_1^3 \frac{1}{x^2} dx$ and the Midpoint approximation?

(A) $\frac{2}{3}$

(B) $\frac{136}{225}$

(C) $\frac{86}{225}$

(D) $\frac{14}{225}$

(E) $\frac{6}{225}$

25. The expression $\frac{1}{4}\left(\left(\frac{1}{4}\right)^2+\left(\frac{2}{4}\right)^2+\left(\frac{3}{4}\right)^2+\left(\frac{4}{4}\right)^2\right)$ is a Right Riemann Sum approximation for

(A) $\int_0^1 \left(\frac{x}{4}\right)^2 dx$

(B) $\int_0^1 x^2 dx$

(C) $\frac{1}{4}\int_0^1 \left(\frac{x}{4}\right)^2 dx$

(D) $\frac{1}{4}\int_0^1 x^2 dx$

(E) $\frac{1}{4}\int_0^4 x^2 dx$

ANSWERS

LIMITS OF FUNCTIONS

DIFFICULTY LEVEL 1

1. **CORRECT ANSWER: B**

    Incorrect answer comments, same for all 4: Factor out the Greatest Common Factor (GCF) from the numerator and denominator, then plug in x = 0.

2. **CORRECT ANSWER: E**

    Incorrect answer comments, same for all 4: Evaluate both parts of the piece-wise function at x = 3. Compare the results to see if the left and right hand limits agree.

3. **CORRECT ANSWER: C**

    Incorrect answer comments, same for all 4: A function is continuous when the limit and the function value agree. In other words, when $\lim_{x \to a} h(x) = h(a)$.

4. **CORRECT ANSWER: E**

    Incorrect answer comments, same for all 4: When the limit at x = 4 results in $\frac{-8}{0}$, plug in values near 4, such as 3.5 and 3.9 from the left, and 4.5 and 4.1 from the right. Observe where the results are heading, and if they are heading to the same value.

5. **CORRECT ANSWER: D**

    Incorrect answer comments, same for all 4: Evaluate the limit at x = π and reduce.

DIFFICULTY LEVEL 2

6. **CORRECT ANSWER: B**

    Incorrect answer comments, same for all 4: Factor the denominator using Difference of Two Squares, simplify, then plug in x = k.

7. **CORRECT ANSWER: A**

   Incorrect answer comments, same for all 4: A limit means as the graph of *f(x)* approaches x = 5 from both left and right, the y-values approach 3. The definition does not state what happens to the graph of *f(x)* at x = 5.

8. **CORRECT ANSWER: B**

   Incorrect answer comments, same for all 4: Multiply the numerator and denominator by the conjugate, then simplify and plug in x = 9.

9. **CORRECT ANSWER: B**

   Incorrect answer comments, same for all 4: Factor the numerator and denominator, simplify, then plug in x = 0.

10. **CORRECT ANSWER: A**

    Incorrect answer comments, same for all 4: The limit of a function exists at a point if both one-sided limits agree. Also, a function is defined at an x-value if a point exists on the graph for that x-value.

11. **CORRECT ANSWER: A**

    Incorrect answer comments, same for all 4: Expand the binomial, simplify, and then evaluate the limit at x = 0.

DIFFICULTY LEVEL 3

12. **CORRECT ANSWER: D**

    Incorrect answer comments, same for all 4: Rewrite each trigonometric function in terms of sin and cos, simplify, and evaluate at x = 1.

13. **CORRECT ANSWER: B**

    Incorrect answer comments, same for all 4: Multiply both terms in the numerator and denominator by the LCD, simplify, and then evaluate at x = 5.

ASYMPTOTIC AND UNBOUNDED BEHAVIOR

DIFFICULTY LEVEL 1

1. **CORRECT ANSWER: A**

   Incorrect answer comments, same for all 4: With limits to infinity, compare only the highest power in numerator and denominator and simplify. Then, analyze the limit.

2. **CORRECT ANSWER: D**

   Incorrect answer comments, same for all 4: With limits to infinity, compare only the highest power in numerator and denominator and simplify. Then, analyze the limit.

3. **CORRECT ANSWER: B**

   Incorrect answer comments, same for all 4:

   Horizontal asymptotes are found when $\lim_{x \to \pm\infty} f(x) = a$.

   Evaluate the limit to negative infinity, and observe how a negative exponent can be rewritten.

4. **CORRECT ANSWER: C**

   Incorrect answer comments, same for all 4: Vertical asymptotes occur when the denominator of a simplified fraction equals zero.

5. **CORRECT ANSWER: C**

   Incorrect answer comments, same for all 4:

   One-sided limits deal with the graph of the function as it approaches from one direction.

   So $\lim_{x \to -2+} f(x)$ is found by describing the graph of f as it approaches from the right side.

DIFFICULTY LEVEL 2

6. **CORRECT ANSWER: E**

    Incorrect answer comments, same for all 4: With limits to infinity, compare only the highest power in numerator and denominator and simplify. Then, analyze the limit.

7. **CORRECT ANSWER: A**

    Incorrect answer comments, same for all 4: With limits to infinity, compare only the highest power in numerator and denominator and simplify. Then, analyze the limit.

8. **CORRECT ANSWER: C**

    Incorrect answer comments, same for all 4: A function has no horizontal asymptote when the values of x increase to each infinity, but the y-values do not converge to any number.

9. **CORRECT ANSWER: B**

    Incorrect answer comments, same for all 4: Vertical asymptotes occur when the denominator of a simplified fraction equals zero.

    Horizontal asymptotes are found when $\lim_{x \to \pm\infty} f(x) = a$.

10. **CORRECT ANSWER: E**

    Incorrect answer comments, same for all 4:

    Vertical asymptotes occur when the denominator of a simplified fraction equals zero.

    Horizontal asymptotes are found when $\lim_{x \to \pm\infty} f(x) = a$.

11. **CORRECT ANSWER: B**

    Incorrect answer comments, same for all 4:

    Vertical asymptotes occur when the one-sided limit of an x-value approaches ∞. Horizontal asymptotes occur when the one-sided limit of as x approaches ∞ is a constant.

DIFFICULTY LEVEL 3

12. CORRECT ANSWER: B

Incorrect answer comments, same for all 4:

Horizontal asymptotes are found when $\lim\limits_{x \to \pm\infty} f(x) = a$.

Evaluate the limit to each infinity, and observe which terms will affect the value of the limit.

CONTINUITY AS A PROPERTY OF FUNCTIONS

DIFFICULTY LEVEL 1

1. **CORRECT ANSWER: B**

   Incorrect answer comments, same for all 4: For all continuous functions, the graph of the function as g approaches each x-value equal to the function value at that point.

2. **CORRECT ANSWER: E**

   Incorrect answer comments, same for all 4: A continuous function is defined for all numbers in its domain. Determine which functions are not defined for certain x-values.

3. **CORRECT ANSWER: E**

   Incorrect answer comments, same for all 4: Continuous functions have limits equal to the function values, but having a limit does not make a function continuous. Continuous functions are defined everywhere in their domain, but having a limit does not guarantee the function is defined everywhere.

4. **CORRECT ANSWER: D**

   Incorrect answer comments, same for all 4: Removable discontinuities occur when common terms can be factored from numerator and denominator. Infinite discontinuities occur when the denominator of a simplified fraction equals zero.

5. **CORRECT ANSWER: C**

   Incorrect answer comments, same for all 4:

   A continuous function has limits at all x-values equal to the function value.

6. **CORRECT ANSWER: C**

   Incorrect answer comments, same for all 4:

   Evaluate the one-sided limit for each part of the piece-wise function using substitution. Also, A function does not exist at an x-value only if no point exists at that x-value.

DIFFICULTY LEVEL 2

7. CORRECT ANSWER: E

Incorrect answer comments, same for all 4:

For continuous functions, $\lim_{x \to 9} f(x) = f(9)$. Find the limit of the function at 9, and set that value equal to k.

8. CORRECT ANSWER: A

Incorrect answer comments, same for all 4:

For continuous functions, $\lim_{x \to 4} g(x) = g(4)$. Find the limit of the function at 4.

9. CORRECT ANSWER: D

Incorrect answer comments, same for all 4: For continuous functions, $\lim_{x \to a^-} f(x) = \lim_{x \to a^+} f(x)$. Determine at which x-values the one-sided limits do not agree.

10. CORRECT ANSWER: E

Incorrect answer comments, same for all 4:

Determine the limit at x = 4, to find the possible y-value to make the function continuous.

DIFFICULTY LEVEL 3

11. CORRECT ANSWER: C

Incorrect answer comments, same for all 4:

For continuous functions at x = 0, $f(0)$ exists. For a function to not be differentiable at x = 0, $f'(0)$ does not exist.

12. CORRECT ANSWER: D

Incorrect answer comments, same for all 4: A function is only continuous if it is defined for all x-values before simplification. Determine which denominator will not result in a function *y* which is undefined.

CONCEPT OF THE DERIVATIVE

DIFFICULTY LEVEL 1

1. **CORRECT ANSWER: B**

   Incorrect answer comments, same for all 4:

   Take the derivative of each term separately, remembering the rules for derivatives of monomials and trigonometric functions.

2. **CORRECT ANSWER: A**

   Incorrect answer comments, same for all 4: Find the derivative of the function, and then evaluate it by plugging in x = If there is no x in the derivative, that is the answer already.

3. **CORRECT ANSWER: A**

   Incorrect answer comments, same for all 4:

   Rewrite $5\sqrt{x}$ as $5x^{\frac{1}{2}}$ and take the derivative of each term separately. Then evaluate it by plugging in x = 4.

4. **CORRECT ANSWER: D**

   Incorrect answer comments, same for all 4: A differentiable function is continuous by definition, along with the statements that are true for continuous functions as well.

5. **CORRECT ANSWER: C**

   Incorrect answer comments, same for all 4:

   First, eliminate all points where the graph is not continuous. For the remaining points, there are three conditions besides a discontinuity that cause a function to be non-differentiable.

6. **CORRECT ANSWER: C**

   Incorrect answer comments, same for all 4:

   If a function has no limit or is not continuous at a point, then it is not differentiable by definition. Also, there are three conditions besides a discontinuity that cause a function to be non-differentiable.

DIFFICULTY LEVEL 2

7. **CORRECT ANSWER: D**

   Incorrect answer comments, same for all 4:

   Rewrite $-\frac{1}{x}$ as $-x^{-1}$ and take the derivative of each term separately. Then evaluate it by plugging in x = 2.

8. **CORRECT ANSWER: E**

   Incorrect answer comments, same for all 4:

   Rewrite $\sqrt[3]{t^4}$ as $t^{\frac{4}{3}}$ and take the derivative using the power rule. Then evaluate it by plugging in x = 8.

9. **CORRECT ANSWER: E**

   Incorrect answer comments, same for all 4:

   Rewrite as three separate fractions and simplify, then take the derivative of each term separately. Last, evaluate it by plugging in x = 1.

10. **CORRECT ANSWER: B**

    Incorrect answer comments, same for all 4:

    Multiply out the expression, then take the derivative of each term separately. Last, evaluate it by plugging in x = -1.

11. **CORRECT ANSWER: B**

   Incorrect answer comments, same for all 4:

   Take the derivative of each term separately, remembering the rules for derivatives of monomials and trigonometric functions. Then, evaluate it by plugging in x = $\frac{\pi}{6}$ and writing as a single fraction.

12. **CORRECT ANSWER: E**

   Incorrect answer comments, same for all 4:

   Rewrite $\left(\frac{1}{x^2} + \frac{1}{\sqrt{x}}\right)$ as $\left(x^{-2} + x^{-\frac{1}{2}}\right)$, then take the derivative of each term separately. Last, evaluate it by plugging in x = 1.

13. **CORRECT ANSWER: B**

   Incorrect answer comments, same for all 4: Evaluate g at x = 0 to determine if it is continuous. Take the derivative of g and evaluate it at x = 0 to determine if it has a derivative.

14. **CORRECT ANSWER: D**

   Incorrect answer comments, same for all 4:

   Evaluate both one-sided limits at x = 4 to determine if the function is continuous there. Take each derivative and evaluate it at x = 4 to determine if it is differentiable there.

15. **CORRECT ANSWER: E**

   Incorrect answer comments, same for all 4:

   The limit definition of a derivative is $f'(x) = \lim_{h \to 0} \frac{f(x+h) - f(x)}{h}$. Rewrite this definition with $f(x) = \log_5 x$ and x = 2.

16. CORRECT ANSWER: C

Incorrect answer comments, same for all 4:

The limit definition of a derivative is $f'(x) = \lim\limits_{h \to 0} \dfrac{f(x+h) - f(x)}{h}$. Identify the function, $f(x)$ and the x-value used in the limit. Take the derivative, then evaluate it at the x-value.

17. CORRECT ANSWER: C

Incorrect answer comments, same for all 4:

The limit definition of a derivative is $f'(x) = \lim\limits_{h \to 0} \dfrac{f(x+h) - f(x)}{h}$. Identify the function, $f(x)$. Take the derivative, then evaluate it at the x-value.

18. CORRECT ANSWER: D

Incorrect answer comments, same for all 4:

The limit definition of a derivative is $f'(x) = \lim\limits_{h \to 0} \dfrac{f(x+h) - f(x)}{h}$. Identify the function, $f(x)$. Then take the derivative.

19. CORRECT ANSWER: E

Incorrect answer comments, same for all 4:

The limit definition of a derivative is $g'(x) = \lim\limits_{h \to 0} \dfrac{g(x+h) - g(x)}{h}$. Also, a differentiable function is also continuous by definition.

DIFFICULTY LEVEL 3

20. CORRECT ANSWER: E

Incorrect answer comments, same for all 4: Evaluate both one-sided limits at x = 1 to determine if the function is continuous there. Take each derivative and evaluate it at x = 1 to determine if it is differentiable there.

21. CORRECT ANSWER: A

Incorrect answer comments, same for all 4: Since f is differentiable, it is also continuous. Find the values of a and b which make both equations equal, and well as their derivatives at x = 1.

DERIVATIVE AT A POINT

DIFFICULTY LEVEL 1

1. **CORRECT ANSWER: B**

    Incorrect answer comments, same for all 4:

    Rewrite $\sqrt[3]{x^4}$ as $x^{\frac{4}{3}}$ and take the derivative using the power rule. Also, remember the rule for taking the derivate of constant terms.

2. **CORRECT ANSWER: E**

    Incorrect answer comments, same for all 4:

    Set he derivatives for each function equal, and solve for x.

3. **CORRECT ANSWER: B**

    Incorrect answer comments, same for all 4:

    Take the derivative of $g(x)$ and evaluate it at x = 1. Remember to use the rules of differentiation of inverse trigonometric functions.

4. **CORRECT ANSWER: E**

    Incorrect answer comments, same for all 4:

    Horizontal tangent lines occur when the derivative equals 0. Set the derivative equal to 0, solve for either coordinate, and plug back into the equation of the curve to find the other coordinate.

5. **CORRECT ANSWER: B**

    Incorrect answer comments, same for all 4:

    Horizontal tangent lines occur when the derivative equals 0. Set the derivative equal to 0, solve for either coordinate, and plug back into the equation of the curve to find the other coordinate.

6. **CORRECT ANSWER: D**

   Incorrect answer comments, same for all 4:

   Vertical tangent lines occur when the derivative is undefined. Set the denominator of the derivative equal to 0, solve for either coordinate, and plug back into the equation of the curve to find the other coordinate.

7. **CORRECT ANSWER: B**

   Incorrect answer comments, same for all 4:

   The equation of a tangent line is given by $y - y_1 = m(x - x_1)$. Find the slope, m, by plugging in the given x_1 value into the derivative.

8. **CORRECT ANSWER: C**

   Incorrect answer comments, same for all 4:

   Find the equation of the tangent line at $x = 2$. Evaluate the tangent line at $x = 2.1$.

DIFFICULTY LEVEL 2

9. **CORRECT ANSWER: A**

   Incorrect answer comments, same for all 4:

   Use Chain Rule to take the derivative, then evaluate the derivative at the given x-value.

10. **CORRECT ANSWER: B**

    Incorrect answer comments, same for all 4:

    Use Chain Rule to take the derivative, then evaluate the derivative at the given x-value.

11. **CORRECT ANSWER: D**

    Incorrect answer comments, same for all 4:

    Set the derivative of $h(x)$ equal to the slope of the line. Solve for x, and then determine when the two graphs intersect to find a.

12. **CORRECT ANSWER: B**

   Incorrect answer comments, same for all 4:

   Set the derivative of y equal to the slope of the line. Solve for x, and find the points where the graphs are tangent to find k.

13. **CORRECT ANSWER: C**

   Incorrect answer comments, same for all 4:

   Set the derivative of $f(x)$ equal to the slope of the line. Solve for x, and then find the point on the graph.

14. **CORRECT ANSWER: A**

   Incorrect answer comments, same for all 4:

   Set the derivative of $f(x)$ equal to the given value and solve for x. Remember to use the Chain Rule when taking the derivative.

15. **CORRECT ANSWER: B**

   Incorrect answer comments, same for all 4:

   Take the derivative of $g(x)$ and evaluate it at x = e. Remember to use the Chain Rule when taking the derivative.

16. **CORRECT ANSWER: C**

   Incorrect answer comments, same for all 4:

   Set the derivative equal to $\frac{1}{4}$, solve for either coordinate, and plug back into the equation of the curve to find the other coordinate.

17. **CORRECT ANSWER: E**

   Incorrect answer comments, same for all 4:

   Horizontal tangents to f occur when $f'(x) = 0$.

18. **CORRECT ANSWER: C**

   Incorrect answer comments, same for all 4:

   Vertical tangent lines occur when the derivative is undefined. Verify which points cause the derivative to be undefined, and also exist on the curve.

19. **CORRECT ANSWER: C**

   Incorrect answer comments, same for all 4:

   Horizontal tangent lines occur when the derivative is 0. Verify which points cause the derivative to be 0, and also exist on the curve.

20. **CORRECT ANSWER: D**

   Incorrect answer comments, same for all 4:

   The equation of a tangent line is given by $y - y_1 = m(x - x_1)$. Find y_1 by plugging in the given x_1 value into the equation. Find the slope, m, by plugging in the given x_1 value into the derivative.

21. **CORRECT ANSWER: A**

   Incorrect answer comments, same for all 4:

   The equation of a tangent line is given by $y - y_1 = m(x - x_1)$. Find y_1 by plugging in the given x_1 value into the equation. Find the slope, m, by plugging in the given x_1 value into the derivative. Remember to use the Chain Rule when differentiation the equation.

22. **CORRECT ANSWER: C**

   Incorrect answer comments, same for all 4:

   The equation of a tangent line is given by $y - y_1 = m(x - x_1)$. Find y_1 by plugging in the given x_1 value into y. Find the slope, m, by plugging in the given x_1 value into the derivative of y. Remember to use the Chain Rule when differentiation the equation.

23. **CORRECT ANSWER: D**

   Incorrect answer comments, same for all 4:

   Find the points on the function f where the derivative is equal to 6. Then write out the equation of the tangent line.

24. CORRECT ANSWER: E

Incorrect answer comments, same for all 4:

The equation of a tangent line is given by $y - y_1 = m(x - x_1)$. Find the slope, m, by plugging in the given x_1 value into the derivative. Remember to use Quotient Rule when taking the derivative.

25. CORRECT ANSWER: C

Incorrect answer comments, same for all 4:

The normal line is perpendicular to the tangent line. Find the equation of the tangent line, and use the negative reciprocal slope for m.

26. CORRECT ANSWER: B

Incorrect answer comments, same for all 4:

Find the equation of the tangent line at x = -1. Evaluate the tangent line at x = -1.1.

27. CORRECT ANSWER: C

Incorrect answer comments, same for all 4:

Find the equation of the tangent line at x = 2. Set the tangent line equal to 0 and solve.

28. CORRECT ANSWER: B

Incorrect answer comments, same for all 4:

Find the equation of the tangent line at x = 4. Evaluate the tangent line at x = 4.4.

29. CORRECT ANSWER: B

Incorrect answer comments, same for all 4:

To approximate $f'(3)$, find the slope of the secant line from x = 2 to 3, and x = 3 to 4. The approximate slope should be in between those two.

DIFFICULTY LEVEL 3

30. CORRECT ANSWER: C

Incorrect answer comments, same for all 4:

Find horizontal and vertical tangents by setting the numerator and denominator equal to 0 respectively. Then find if the curve has points with those coordinates. When x = 4, find possible y-values on the curve, and determine the slope at those points.

31. CORRECT ANSWER: A

Incorrect answer comments, same for all 4:

Find horizontal and vertical tangents by setting the numerator and denominator equal to 0 respectively. To find the derivative, use Implicit Differentiation or solve the equation for y and use the Quotient Rule.

32. CORRECT ANSWER: E

Incorrect answer comments, same for all 4:

The equation of a tangent line is given by $y - y_1 = m(x - x_1)$. Find y_1 by plugging in the given x_1 value into $h(x)$. Find the slope, m, by plugging in the given x_1 value into the derivative of $h(x)$. Remember to use the Product Rule when differentiation the equation.

33. **CORRECT ANSWER: D**

   Incorrect answer comments, same for all 4:

   The equation of a tangent line is given by $y - y_1 = m(x - x_1)$. Find the slope, m, by plugging in the given x_1 value into the derivative. Remember to use Product and Chain Rule when taking the derivative, or expand the expression before taking the derivative.

34. **CORRECT ANSWER: A**

   Incorrect answer comments, same for all 4:

   Find the derivative of the curve using Implicit Differentiation. Vertical tangent lines exist when the derivative is undefined. Set the denominator equal to 0, and find the coordinates for x and y.

35. **CORRECT ANSWER: A**

   Incorrect answer comments, same for all 4:

   The normal line is perpendicular to the tangent line. Find the equation of the tangent line, and use the negative reciprocal slope for m. Also, remember to use the Chain Rule when taking the derivative.

36. **CORRECT ANSWER: E**

   Incorrect answer comments, same for all 4:

   The normal line is perpendicular to the tangent line. Find the equation of the tangent line, and use the negative reciprocal slope for m.

37. **CORRECT ANSWER: D**

   Incorrect answer comments, same for all 4:

   The normal line is perpendicular to the tangent line. Find the equation of the tangent line, and use the negative reciprocal slope for m. Remember to use the Chain Rule when finding the derivative.

38. **CORRECT ANSWER: A**

   Incorrect answer comments, same for all 4:

   Find the equation of the tangent line at x = 2. Set x and y equal to k, and solve.

39. CORRECT ANSWER: B

Incorrect answer comments, same for all 4:

To approximate the shark's position at t = 3.5, find the tangent lines at t = 3 and t = 4, where P gives the value of y_1, and $\dfrac{P}{t}$ gives m. Approximate t = 3.5 in each tangent line, since P and P' are increasing, the true approximation is in between those two.

Derivative at a Point

DERIVATIVE AS A FUNCTION

DIFFICULTY LEVEL 1

1. **CORRECT ANSWER: C**

   Incorrect answer comments, same for all 4:

   Functions have a minimum value when the derivate changes from negative to positive. Take the derivate of g. Find where $g'(x) = 0$, then plug in x-values on either side of the zeroes to see if the derivative changes from negative (decreasing) to positive (increasing).

2. **CORRECT ANSWER: B**

   Incorrect answer comments, same for all 4:

   Functions are increasing when the derivate is positive. Take the derivate of f. Find where $f'(x) = 0$, then plug in x-values on either side of the zeroes to see where the derivative is positive (increasing).

3. **CORRECT ANSWER: E**

   Incorrect answer comments, same for all 4:

   Functions have a maximum value when the derivate changes from positive to negative. Take the derivate of g. Find where $g'(x) = 0$, then plug in x-values on either side of the zeroes to see if the derivative changes from positive (increasing) to negative (decreasing).

4. **CORRECT ANSWER: D**

   Incorrect answer comments, same for all 4:

   At a maximum value, the derivate changes from positive to negative. At a minimum value, the derivate changes from negative to positive. Also, at any relative extrema on a differentiable function, the derivative equals 0. If necessary, sketch a graph to observe the behavior of h.

5. **CORRECT ANSWER: C**

   Incorrect answer comments, same for all 4:

Functions are decreasing when the derivate is positive. Take the derivate of f. Find where $f'(x) = 0$, then plug in x-values on either side of the zeroes to see where the derivative is negative (decreasing).

6. **CORRECT ANSWER: C**

    Incorrect answer comments, same for all 4:

    Functions are increasing when the derivate is positive. Analyze the data in the table to find when f' is positive, thus f is increasing.

7. **CORRECT ANSWER: E**

    Incorrect answer comments, same for all 4:

    Functions have a minimum value when the derivate changes from negative to positive. Remember that the graph shown above is of the derivative of f. Find where $f'(x) = 0$, and notice when the derivative changes from negative to positive.

8. **CORRECT ANSWER: B**

    Incorrect answer comments, same for all 4:

    Functions are decreasing when the derivate is negative. Remember that the graph shown above is of the derivative of f. Find all intervals where $f'(x)$ is negative.

9. **CORRECT ANSWER: E**

    Incorrect answer comments, same for all 4:

    If $f'(x) > 0$ everywhere except x = 0, then f is increasing everywhere but at x = 0. Determine which graphs of f are increasing everywhere.

DIFFICULTY LEVEL 2

10. CORRECT ANSWER: B

Incorrect answer comments, same for all 4:

Functions have a maximum value when the derivate changes from positive to negative. Expand the expression and take the derivate of f. Find where $f'(x) = 0$, then plug in x-values on either side of the zeroes to see if the derivative changes from positive (increasing) to negative (decreasing).

11. CORRECT ANSWER: B

Incorrect answer comments, same for all 4:

Functions have a maximum value when the derivate changes from positive to negative. Since the derivative is given, $f'(x) = 0$ at x = 1, 2, 3, and 4. Plug in x-values on either side of the zeroes to see if the derivative changes from positive (increasing) to negative (decreasing).

12. CORRECT ANSWER: A

Incorrect answer comments, same for all 4:

At a maximum value, the derivate changes from positive to negative. At a minimum value, the derivate changes from negative to positive. Plug in x-values on either side of the zeroes to see if the derivative changes sign.

13. CORRECT ANSWER: D

Incorrect answer comments, same for all 4:

Take the derivative of f and set it equal to 0. Remember to use the Product Rule. Since h is always negative and h' is always positive, plug in x-values on either side of the zero to see the behavior of the graph.

14. CORRECT ANSWER: A

Incorrect answer comments, same for all 4:

Functions are increasing when the derivate is positive. Take the derivate of f. Remember to use the Product Rule. Find where $f'(x) = 0$, then plug in x-values on either side of the zeroes to see where the derivative is positive (increasing).

15. CORRECT ANSWER: B

Incorrect answer comments, same for all 4:

Take the derivate of g. Remember to use the Product Rule. Find $g'(1)$, and if it is positive or negative, then g is increasing or decreasing respectively. If $g'(1) = 0$, then plug in x-values on either side to see if the derivative changes from positive to negative (maximum) or negative to positive (minimum).

16. CORRECT ANSWER: B

Incorrect answer comments, same for all 4:

Functions are increasing when the derivate is positive. Find where $f'(x) = 0$ or undefined, then plug in x-values on either side of the zeroes to see where the derivative is positive (increasing).

17. CORRECT ANSWER: C

Incorrect answer comments, same for all 4:

Remember that the graph shown above is of the derivative of f. Functions have a maximum value when the derivate changes from positive to negative, and vice versa for minimums. Functions are increasing when the derivate is positive, and decreasing when the derivative is negative. Also, if the graph of the derivative of f is continuous, then it is defined for all points in the interval.

18. CORRECT ANSWER: A

Incorrect answer comments, same for all 4:

When $f'(x) > 0$, f will be increasing. When $f'(x) < 0$, f will be decreasing. Match up the intervals of the graph of $f'(x)$ with the corresponding intervals of the graph of f.

19. CORRECT ANSWER: D

Incorrect answer comments, same for all 4:

When f is increasing, $f'(x) > 0$. When f is decreasing, $f'(x) < 0$. Match up the intervals of the graph of f with the corresponding intervals of the graph of $f'(x)$.

DIFFICULTY LEVEL 3

20. CORRECT ANSWER: D

Incorrect answer comments, same for all 4:

Functions have a maximum value when the derivate changes from positive to negative. Ignoring the absolute value, take the derivative of h and set it equal to zero. The maximum occurs either at this point, or one of the endpoints of the domain. Plug each into the equation for h to find the maximum value.

21. CORRECT ANSWER: A

Incorrect answer comments, same for all 4:

Functions are decreasing when the derivate is negative. Remember that the graph shown above is of the derivative of f. Find the derivative of h and determine what values of f make h' negative.

SECOND DERIVATIVES

DIFFICULTY LEVEL 1

1. **CORRECT ANSWER: C**

   Incorrect answer comments, same for all 4:

   Functions are concave up when the second derivate is positive. Take the second derivate of f. Find where $f''(x) = 0$, then plug in x-values on either side of the zeroes to see where the second derivative is positive (concave up).

2. **CORRECT ANSWER: C**

   Incorrect answer comments, same for all 4:

   Functions have a point of inflection when the second derivate changes sign. Find where $f''(x) = 0$, then plug in x-values on either side of the zeroes to see if the second derivative changes sign.

3. **CORRECT ANSWER: C**

   Incorrect answer comments, same for all 4:

   Functions have a point of inflection when the second derivate changes sign, not just when the second derivative equals 0. Determine how many times f'' changes sign in the table.

4. **CORRECT ANSWER: A**

   Incorrect answer comments, same for all 4:

   When a graph is concave up, the slope increases. A simple graph that is always concave up is the graph of the parabola $y = x^2$.

5. **CORRECT ANSWER: B**

   Incorrect answer comments, same for all 4:

   The graph of f is increasing, so the first derivative is positive. The graph of f is concave down, so the second derivative is negative. $f(k) = 0$ since it is an x-intercept of the graph.

6. **CORRECT ANSWER: C**

   Incorrect answer comments, same for all 4:

   If y' changes sign, the y shifts from increasing to decreasing or vice versa. If y'' does not change sign, then y is either always concave up or concave down. Find the graph that fits both criteria.

   DIFFICULTY LEVEL 2

7. **CORRECT ANSWER: E**

   Incorrect answer comments, same for all 4:

   Functions have a point of inflection when the second derivate changes sign. Take the second derivate of f. Find where $f''(x) = 0$, then plug in x-values on either side of the zeroes to see if the second derivative changes sign.

8. **CORRECT ANSWER: A**

   Incorrect answer comments, same for all 4:

   Functions are concave down when the second derivate is negative. Take the second derivate of y. Find where $y''(x) = 0$, then plug in x-values on either side of the zeroes to see where the second derivative is negative (concave down).

9. **CORRECT ANSWER: B**

   Incorrect answer comments, same for all 4:

   Find where $\dfrac{d^2 y}{dx^2} = 0$, then plug in x-values on either side of the zeroes to see where the second derivative is negative (concave down), and to see where it changes sign for points of inflection.

10. **CORRECT ANSWER: C**

    Incorrect answer comments, same for all 4:

    Functions have a point of inflection when the second derivate changes sign. Take the second derivate of f. Find where $f''(x) = 0$, then plug in x-values on either side of the zeroes to see if the second derivative changes sign.

11. CORRECT ANSWER: C

Incorrect answer comments, same for all 4:

Functions have a point of inflection when the second derivate changes sign. Take the second derivative remembering to use the Quotient Rule, and find where $\frac{d^2 y}{dx^2} = 0$. Plug in x-values on either side of the zeroes to see where the second derivative changes sign for points of inflection. Ignore points that that y is not defined at.

12. CORRECT ANSWER: A

Incorrect answer comments, same for all 4:

Take the second derivate of g, and find where $g''(x) = 0$, then plug in x-values on either side of the zeroes to identify the x-value for the point of inflection. Plug this x into g and g' to find the y-value and slope of the tangent line, respectively.

13. CORRECT ANSWER: E

Incorrect answer comments, same for all 4:

Take the second derivate of f, and find where $g''(x) = 0$. Plug this x-value into f' to find the slope of the tangent line, and then use the negative reciprocal slope for the normal line.

14. CORRECT ANSWER: E

Incorrect answer comments, same for all 4:

Functions are concave up when the second derivative is positive, which is the slope of the first derivative. Remember that the graph shown above is of the derivative of f. Find all intervals where the slope of $f'(x)$ is positive.

15. CORRECT ANSWER: B

Incorrect answer comments, same for all 4:

Remember that the graph shown above is of the second derivative of f. f' increasing means that f is concave up, which means f'' is positive. Identify the intervals of the graph where $f'' > 0$.

16. CORRECT ANSWER: B

Incorrect answer comments, same for all 4:

When $f''(x) > 0$, f will be concave up. When $f''(x) < 0$, f will be concave down. Match up the intervals of the graph of $f''(x)$ with the corresponding intervals of the graph of f.

17. CORRECT ANSWER: D

Incorrect answer comments, same for all 4:

When comparing f' and f'', it is the same as comparing f and f'. With that in mind, when f is increasing, $f'(x) > 0$. When f is decreasing, $f'(x) < 0$. Match up the intervals of the graph of f with the corresponding intervals of the graph of $f'(x)$.

18. CORRECT ANSWER: E

Incorrect answer comments, same for all 4:

If $f' < 0$ and $f'' < 0$, then the graph of f must be decreasing and concave down. Identify any intervals than fit both criteria.

DIFFICULTY LEVEL 3

19. CORRECT ANSWER: D

Incorrect answer comments, same for all 4:

Functions are concave up when the second derivate is positive. Take the second derivate of f. Remember to use the Quotient Rule. Find where $f''(x) = 0$ or undefined, then plug in x-values on either side of the zeroes to see where the second derivative is positive (concave up).

20. CORRECT ANSWER: E

Incorrect answer comments, same for all 4:

Take the second derivate of f. Remember to use the Chain Rule. Since f has a point of inflection at x=1, then $f''(1) = 0$. Solve the equation for a, then evaluate $f''(0)$.

21. CORRECT ANSWER: B

Incorrect answer comments, same for all 4:

Functions are concave up when the second derivative is positive. Remember that the graph shown above is of the derivative of f. Find the second derivative of g using the Chain Rule, and determine what the signs of f and f' are at each point.

APPLICATIONS OF DERIVATIVES

DIFFICULTY LEVEL 1

1. **CORRECT ANSWER: D**

   Incorrect answer comments, same for all 4:

   The Related Rates formula required here is the area of a square, $A = s^2$. Take the derivate of this equation using Implicit Differentiation to get $\frac{dA}{dt} = 2s\frac{ds}{dt}$. Plug in the value of the variables after the derivative is taken, not before, and solve for the change of area, $\frac{dA}{dt}$.

2. **CORRECT ANSWER: C**

   Incorrect answer comments, same for all 4:

   The Related Rates formula required here is the area of a circle, $A = \pi r^2$, and the diameter of a circle, $D = 2r$. Take the derivate of the area and diameter using Implicit Differentiation to get $\frac{dA}{dt} = 2\pi r \frac{dr}{dt}$ and $\frac{dD}{dt} = 2\frac{dr}{dt}$. Since the area increases twice as fast as the diameter, which increases twice as fast as the radius, replace $\frac{dA}{dt}$ with an equal expression in terms of $\frac{dr}{dt}$. Simplify the equation and solve for the radius, r.

3. **CORRECT ANSWER: A**

   Incorrect answer comments, same for all 4:

   For inverse functions, since $g(-3) = 2$, then $g^{-1}(2) = -3$. The Inverse Derivative Formula states $(g^{-1})'(y) = \frac{1}{g'(x)}$. Plug in the x-value when y = 2 into the formula and simplify.

4. **CORRECT ANSWER: A**

    Incorrect answer comments, same for all 4:

    For inverse functions, since $g(18) = 2$, then the Inverse Derivative Formula states $g'(18) = \dfrac{1}{f'(2)}$. Find the derivative of f and evaluate at the given x-value.

5. **CORRECT ANSWER: C**

    Incorrect answer comments, same for all 4:

    For inverse functions, since $g(18) = f(c)$, for some value of c, then determine the value of c by setting f equal to -3. The Inverse Derivative Formula states $g'(18) = \dfrac{1}{f'(c)}$. Find the derivative of f and evaluate at c.

6. **CORRECT ANSWER: D**

    Incorrect answer comments, same for all 4:

    Velocity is the first derivative of position. Find $v(t) = p'(t)$, set equal to 0 and solve for t.

7. **CORRECT ANSWER: D**

    Incorrect answer comments, same for all 4:

    Velocity is the first derivative of position. When an object is at rest, the velocity of that object is zero. Find $v(t) = p'(t)$, set equal to 0 and solve for t.

8. **CORRECT ANSWER: B**

    Incorrect answer comments, same for all 4:

    Velocity is the first derivative of position. An object is moving to the right when the velocity is positive. Find where $v(t) = p'(t) = 0$, then plug in x-values on either side of the zeroes to see where the velocity is positive.

9. **CORRECT ANSWER: D**

   Incorrect answer comments, same for all 4:

   Average velocity is the change in distance over change in time. Find the average velocity from 0 to 2 using and simplify.

10. **CORRECT ANSWER: C**

    Incorrect answer comments, same for all 4:

    Acceleration is the first derivative of velocity, so acceleration is negative when the graph of velocity has a negative slope. Determine when the graph of velocity ha2s a slope that is negative.

11. **CORRECT ANSWER: D**

    Incorrect answer comments, same for all 4:

    An object changes directions when the velocity changes sign. Since the graph shows the velocity, determine when the graph changes from positive to negative, or vice versa.

DIFFICULTY LEVEL 2

12. **CORRECT ANSWER: C**

    Incorrect answer comments, same for all 4:

    The Related Rates formula required here is the area of a rectangle, $A = xy$. Take the derivate of this equation using Implicit Differentiation to get $\frac{dA}{dt} = x\frac{dy}{dt} + y\frac{dx}{dt}$. Plug in the value of the variables after the derivative is taken, not before, and solve for the change of area, $\frac{dA}{dt}$. Also, recall that changes that are decreasing mean the rate is negative.

13. **CORRECT ANSWER: D**

   Incorrect answer comments, same for all 4:

   The Related Rates formula required here are both given. Take the derivate of both using Implicit Differentiation and set them equal to get $4\pi r^2 \dfrac{dr}{dt} = 8\pi r \dfrac{dr}{dt}$. Plug in the value of the variables after the derivative is taken, not before, and solve for the radius, r.

14. **CORRECT ANSWER: A**

   Incorrect answer comments, same for all 4:

   The Related Rates formula required here, in addition to volume, is $C = 2\pi r$. Take the derivate of volume using Implicit Differentiation to get $\dfrac{dV}{dt} = 4\pi r^2 \dfrac{dr}{dt}$. Plug in the value of the variables after the derivative is taken, not before, and solve for the change of radius, $\dfrac{dr}{dt}$. The derivative of the circumference formula, $\dfrac{dC}{dt} = 2\pi \dfrac{dr}{dt}$, is now used to find the change in circumference.

15. **CORRECT ANSWER: B**

   Incorrect answer comments, same for all 4:

   The Related Rates formula required here is the area of a triangle, $A = \dfrac{1}{2} bh$. Take the derivate of this equation using Implicit Differentiation to get $\dfrac{dA}{dt} = \dfrac{1}{2}\left(b\dfrac{dh}{dt} + h\dfrac{db}{dt}\right)$. Use the ratios of the rates of change and the equality of the dimensions to reduce the number of different variables, and solve for either b or h.

16. CORRECT ANSWER: D

Incorrect answer comments, same for all 4:

The Related Rates formula required here is given. Take the derivate of volume using Implicit Differentiation to get $\frac{dV}{dt} = \frac{1}{3}\pi\left(r^2\frac{dh}{dt} + 2rh\frac{dr}{dt}\right)$. Plug in the value of the variables after the derivative is taken, not before, and solve for the change of volume, $\frac{dV}{dt}$. Remember, the sign of the rate of change indicates if the change is an increase of decrease.

17. CORRECT ANSWER: B

Incorrect answer comments, same for all 4:

The Related Rates formula required here is the Pythagorean Theorem, $x^2 + y^2 = z^2$. Take the derivate of the formula using Implicit Differentiation to get $x\frac{dx}{dt} + y\frac{dy}{dt} = z\frac{dz}{dt}$ after simplifying. Plug in the value of the variables after the derivative is taken, not before, and solve for the change of the height of the ladder, $\frac{dy}{dt}$. Remember, since the length of the ladder does not change, $\frac{dz}{dt} = 0$.

18. CORRECT ANSWER: C

Incorrect answer comments, same for all 4:

The Related Rates formula required here is given. Take the derivate of volume using Implicit Differentiation to get $\frac{dV}{dt} = \pi r^2 \frac{dh}{dt}$. Since the radius does not change, the Product Rule does not apply to taking the derivative. Plug in the value of the variables after the derivative is taken, not before, and solve for the change of volume, $\frac{dV}{dt}$.

19. CORRECT ANSWER: B

Incorrect answer comments, same for all 4:

For inverse functions, since $f(-3) = 2$, then $f^{-1}(2) = -3$. The Inverse Derivative Formula states $(f^{-1})'(2) = \dfrac{1}{f'(-3)}$. The slope found by $(f^{-1})'(2)$ is of the tangent line, the normal line will have a negative reciprocal slope.

20. CORRECT ANSWER: A

Incorrect answer comments, same for all 4:

Since the graph of the function f^{-1} contains the point $(1,5)$, then f must contain $(5,1)$. The Inverse Derivative Formula states $(f^{-1})'(1) = \dfrac{1}{f'(5)}$. The value of $(f^{-1})'(1)$ is known, so find $f'(5)$ and plug all values into the formula for the tangent line, $y - y_1 = m(x - x_1)$.

21. CORRECT ANSWER: E

Incorrect answer comments, same for all 4:

Acceleration is the second derivative of position. Find $a(t) = x''(t)$, and evaluate it at $t = 3$.

22. CORRECT ANSWER: C

Incorrect answer comments, same for all 4:

Acceleration is the first derivative of velocity. Find $a(t) = v'(t)$, set it equal to 2 and solve for t. Plug this value of t into the velocity equation.

23. CORRECT ANSWER: A

Incorrect answer comments, same for all 4:

Velocity is the first derivative of position, and acceleration is the first derivative of velocity. Find where $v(t) = 0$, then plug in x-values on either side of the zeroes to see where the velocity is negative. Then, find where $a(t) = 0$, then plug in x-values on either side of the zeroes to see where the acceleration is positive. Determine which intervals are common between the two.

24. CORRECT ANSWER: D

Incorrect answer comments, same for all 4:

Acceleration is the first derivative of velocity. To find the maximum of the acceleration graph, take the derivative of $a(t)$, and set it equal to zero. Those critical x-values and the endpoints of the intervals must be plugged in to the acceleration function to see at which the maximum value occurs.

25. CORRECT ANSWER: C

Incorrect answer comments, same for all 4:

The speed on an object is increasing when velocity and acceleration have the same signs. An object is moving right when the velocity is positive, and it stops moving when the velocity is zero. Compare the values for velocity and acceleration to determine which is correct.

26. CORRECT ANSWER: D

Incorrect answer comments, same for all 4:

Velocity is the first derivative of position, so the velocity is positive when the slope of the position graph is positive. The velocity is negative when the slope of the position graph is negative. Determine when velocity should be positive and negative on the position graph, and identify which velocity graph is positive and negative over the same intervals.

27. CORRECT ANSWER: C

Incorrect answer comments, same for all 4:

An object changes directions when the velocity changes sign. Since the graph shows the velocity, when the graph is below the x-axis, the particle is moving left, and when the graph is above the x-axis, it is moving right. Determine the time when the particle stops moving to the left.

DIFFICULTY LEVEL 3

28. CORRECT ANSWER: E

Incorrect answer comments, same for all 4:

The Related Rates formula required here is the area of a rectangle, $A = xy$. Take the derivate of this equation using Implicit Differentiation, and substitute in $\frac{dA}{dt} = 0$. Then determine which equation is equivalent.

29. CORRECT ANSWER: E

Incorrect answer comments, same for all 4:

The Related Rates formula required here is the Trigonometric Function, $\tan\theta = \frac{y}{x}$. Take the derivate of the formula using Implicit Differentiation to get $\sec^2\theta \frac{d\theta}{dt} = \frac{x\frac{dy}{dt} - y\frac{dx}{dt}}{x^2}$. Plug in the value of the variables after the derivative is taken, not before, and solve for the change of the angle, $\frac{d\theta}{dt}$. Remember, to find the value of $\sec^2\theta$, use the SOH-CAH-TOA proportions in the right triangle.

30. CORRECT ANSWER: E

Incorrect answer comments, same for all 4:

Velocity is the first derivative of position, and acceleration is the first derivative of velocity. Find all values of c where $v(c) = -2$ and $a(c) = \pm 3$. Plug these values of c into the position equation.

31. CORRECT ANSWER: C

Incorrect answer comments, same for all 4:

Velocity is the first derivative of position, and acceleration is the first derivative of velocity. Find $v(t)$ and $a(t)$, set the equations equal, and solve for t. Remember, the only solutions required are in the given time interval of $[0, 10]$.

32. CORRECT ANSWER: D

Incorrect answer comments, same for all 4:

Velocity is the first derivative of position. To find the minimum of the velocity graph, take the derivative of $v(t)$, and set it equal to zero. Then plug in x-values on either side of the zeroes to see if the point is a minimum. Remember, when taking the derivative of the position function, use Chain Rule.

33. CORRECT ANSWER: B

Incorrect answer comments, same for all 4:

Acceleration is the first derivative of velocity. To find the maximum and minimum of the acceleration graph, take the derivative of $a(t)$, and set it equal to zero. Those critical x-values and the endpoints of the intervals must be plugged in to the acceleration function to see at which the maximum and minimum occurs. Subtract the minimum from the maximum to find the difference.

34. CORRECT ANSWER: E

Incorrect answer comments, same for all 4:

The speed on an object is increasing when velocity and acceleration have the same sign. Find $v(t)$ and $a(t)$, and determine when they are either both positive or both negative. Remember, the only solutions required are in the given time interval of [0, 5].

35. CORRECT ANSWER: C

Incorrect answer comments, same for all 4:

The speed on an object is decreasing when velocity and acceleration have opposite signs. Find $v(t)$ and $a(t)$, and determine the time when one is positive and the other is negative. Remember, the only solutions required are in the given time interval of [0, 10].

COMPUTATION OF DERIVATIVES

PART 1

DIFFICULTY LEVEL 1

1. **CORRECT ANSWER: A**

   Incorrect answer comments, same for all 4:

   Rewrite the expression as $(3x + x^{-1} - x^{-2})$, then take the derivative using the Power Rule. Evaluate the derivative at x = -1.

2. **CORRECT ANSWER: C**

   Incorrect answer comments, same for all 4:

   Since the exponential function and the natural logarithmic function are inverses, the function g simplifies into $g(x) = x^2$. Take the derivative using the Power Rule.

3. **CORRECT ANSWER: C**

   Incorrect answer comments, same for all 4:

   Take the derivative using the rule for exponentials, which says $(a^x)' = a^x \ln a$. Evaluate the derivative at x = 2.

4. **CORRECT ANSWER: E**

   Incorrect answer comments, same for all 4:

   Take the derivative of each term separately. Use the rules for derivatives of Trigonometric Functions, which says $(\sin x)' = \cos x$ and $(\tan x)' = \sec^2 x$

DIFFICULTY LEVEL 2

5. CORRECT ANSWER: C

Incorrect answer comments, same for all 4:

Take the derivative using the Product Rule, which says $(f \bullet g)' = f \bullet g' + f' \bullet g$. Also, be sure to use the fact that $(\ln x)' = \dfrac{1}{x}$.

6. CORRECT ANSWER: D

Incorrect answer comments, same for all 4:

Rewrite the expression as $2x(3-x)^{\frac{1}{2}}$, and take the derivative using the Product Rule, which says $(f \bullet g)' = f \bullet g' + f' \bullet g$. When taking the derivative of $(3-x)^{\frac{1}{2}}$, the Chain Rule must also be used, which says $(f(g))' = f'(g) \bullet g'$. The outer function is the radical, and the inner function is the (3-x). Simplify the result by obtaining a common denominator and reducing.

7. CORRECT ANSWER: A

Incorrect answer comments, same for all 4:

Take the derivative using the Chain Rule, which says $(f(g))' = f'(g) \bullet g'$. The outer function is the exponent, and the inner function is the polynomial. Evaluate the derivative at x = 2.

8. CORRECT ANSWER: B

Incorrect answer comments, same for all 4:

Take the derivative using the Chain Rule, which says $(f(g))' = f'(g) \bullet g'$. The outer function is the exponent, and the inner function is the natural log. Also, be sure to use the fact that $(\ln x)' = \dfrac{1}{x}$. Evaluate the derivative at x = e.

9. **CORRECT ANSWER: D**

   Incorrect answer comments, same for all 4:

   Take the derivative using the Quotient Rule, which says $(\frac{f}{g})' = \frac{g \bullet f' - f \bullet g'}{(g')^2}$. Simplify the result by combining like terms.

10. **CORRECT ANSWER: B**

    Incorrect answer comments, same for all 4:

    Take the derivative using the Quotient Rule, which says $(\frac{f}{g})' = \frac{g \bullet f' - f \bullet g'}{(g')^2}$. Evaluate the derivative at x = -1.

11. **CORRECT ANSWER: D**

    Incorrect answer comments, same for all 4:

    Rewrite all trigonometric functions in terms of sine and cosine, so that $f(x) = \cos x (\frac{1}{\cos x} + \frac{\sin x}{\cos x})$. Distribute and simplify first, and then take the derivative

12. **CORRECT ANSWER: D**

    Incorrect answer comments, same for all 4:

    Take the derivative using the Quotient Rule, which says $(\frac{f}{g})' = \frac{g \bullet f' - f \bullet g'}{(g')^2}$. Also, be sure to use the fact that $(\ln x)' = \frac{1}{x}$.

13. **CORRECT ANSWER: A**

    Incorrect answer comments, same for all 4:

    Take the derivative using the Product Rule, which says $(f \bullet g)' = f \bullet g' + f' \bullet g$. When taking the derivative, remember the rule for exponentials, which says $(a^x)' = a^x \ln a$. Evaluate the derivative at x = 0.

14. **CORRECT ANSWER: E**

    Incorrect answer comments, same for all 4:

Take the derivative using the Chain Rule, which says $(f(g))' = f'(g) \bullet g'$. The outer function is the trigonometric and the inner function is the monomial. After taking the first derivative and simplifying, take the second derivative.

15. CORRECT ANSWER: A

Incorrect answer comments, same for all 4:

Take the derivative using the Chain Rule, which says $(f(g))' = f'(g) \bullet g'$. The outer function is the exponent and the inner function is the binomial. Repeat this process two more times, and plug in x = 0, if there is an x term remaining. If not, then the answer is already there.

16. CORRECT ANSWER: B

Incorrect answer comments, same for all 4:

Take the derivative using the Product Rule, which says $(f \bullet g)' = f \bullet g' + f' \bullet g$. The Chain Rule must also be used when taking the derivative of $(x-3)^2$. Evaluate the derivative at x = 2.

17. CORRECT ANSWER: D

Incorrect answer comments, same for all 4:

Rewrite the equation as $g(x) = \ln e - \ln(x^2 - 5x)$ using the laws of logarithms. This simplifies into $g(x) = 1 - \ln(x^2 - 5x)$. Take the derivative using the Chain Rule and simplify.

18. CORRECT ANSWER: D

Incorrect answer comments, same for all 4:

Take the derivative of the left side using the Chain Rule, which says $(f(g))' = f'(g) \bullet g'$. Take the derivative of the right side by rewriting $\frac{1}{x} = x^{-1}$ and using the Power Rule. Plug in all of the values given for each function at the x-values, and solve for $g'(0.5)$.

19. CORRECT ANSWER: E

Incorrect answer comments, same for all 4:

Substitute in for u in the original equation, and take the derivative using the Chain Rule, which says $(f(g))' = f'(g) \bullet g'$. Evaluate the derivative at $x = \dfrac{\pi}{3}$.

20. CORRECT ANSWER: A

Incorrect answer comments, same for all 4:

Take the derivative using the Chain Rule, which says $(f(g))' = f'(g) \bullet g'$. Use the rules for derivatives of Inverse Trigonometric Functions, which says $(\arctan x)' = \dfrac{1}{1+x^2}$.

DIFFICULTY LEVEL 3

21. CORRECT ANSWER: A

Incorrect answer comments, same for all 4:

Take the derivative using the Chain Rule, which says $(f(g))' = f'(g) \bullet g'$. The Chain Rule must be applied twice, since there are three functions present. The outer function is the exponent, the middle function is the trigonometric, and the inner function is the monomial.

22. CORRECT ANSWER: C

Incorrect answer comments, same for all 4:

Take the derivative using the Chain Rule, which says $(f(g))' = f'(g) \bullet g'$. The Chain Rule must be applied twice, since there are three functions present. The outer function is the trigonometric, the middle function is the exponential, and the inner function is the monomial.

23. CORRECT ANSWER: C

Incorrect answer comments, same for all 4:

Take the derivative using the Quotient Rule, which says $\left(\dfrac{f}{g}\right)' = \dfrac{g \bullet f' - f \bullet g'}{(g')^2}$. Plug in the given values of the functions when $x = -1$, and solve for $g(-1)$.

24. CORRECT ANSWER: C

Incorrect answer comments, same for all 4:

Rewrite the expression as $(\sin(\pi x))^{\frac{1}{3}}$, and take the derivative using the Chain Rule, which says $(f(g))' = f'(g) \bullet g'$. The Chain Rule must be applied twice, since there are three functions present. The outer function is the exponent, the middle function is the trigonometric, and the inner function is the monomial.

25. CORRECT ANSWER: D

Incorrect answer comments, same for all 4:

Take the derivative using the Quotient Rule, which says $(\frac{f}{g})' = \frac{g \bullet f' - f \bullet g'}{(g')^2}$. The Chain Rule must also be used when taking the derivative of $(g(x))^2$. Plug in all of the values given for each function at x = 2, and solve for k.

26. CORRECT ANSWER: C

Incorrect answer comments, same for all 4:

Take the derivative using the Chain Rule, which says $(f(g))' = f'(g) \bullet g'$. Use the rules for derivatives of Inverse Trigonometric Functions, which says $(\arcsin x)' = \frac{1}{\sqrt{1-x^2}}$. Remember, to evaluate $\arcsin \frac{1}{2}$, it is the same as solving $\sin \theta = \frac{1}{2}$

27. CORRECT ANSWER: D

Incorrect answer comments, same for all 4:

Take the derivative using the Chain Rule, which says $(f(g))' = f'(g) \bullet g'$. Use the rules for derivatives of Inverse Trigonometric Functions, which says $(\arccos x)' = -\frac{1}{\sqrt{1-x^2}}$. Also, since any trigonometric function and its "arc" counterpart are inverses, when they are composed together, they cancel out, leaving only the variable

PART 2

DIFFICULTY LEVEL 1

1. CORRECT ANSWER: B

Incorrect answer comments, same for all 4:

Take the derivative using Implicit Differentiation, which says take the derivative of x and y as if they were separate functions. Whenever the derivative of a y term is taken, the result is $\frac{dy}{dx}$. For this example, the derivate is $x(\frac{dy}{dx}) + 1 \cdot y - 3x^2 = 0$. Solve for $\frac{dy}{dx}$ and evaluate at the given point.

2. CORRECT ANSWER: B

Incorrect answer comments, same for all 4:

The slopes in the slope field only change when the x-value changes, not when the y-value changes. So the differential equation that corresponds to this slope field can not have a y-variable. Also, for $x > 0$, $\frac{dy}{dx}$ must be positive, since the slopes are positive. For $x < 0$, $\frac{dy}{dx}$ must be negative, since the slopes are negative.

3. CORRECT ANSWER: C

Incorrect answer comments, same for all 4:

The slopes in the slope field are 0 when $y = 2$. So the differential equation that corresponds to this slope field must be 0 when $y = 2$. Also, for $y < 2$, $\frac{dy}{dx}$ must be positive, since the slopes are positive. For $y > 2$, $\frac{dy}{dx}$ must be negative, since the slopes are negative.

4. CORRECT ANSWER: E

Incorrect answer comments, same for all 4:

The slopes in the slope field change when either the x-value changes or y-value changes. So the differential equation that corresponds to this slope field contains both variables.

Also, the slopes in the slope field are 0 when $y = x$. So the differential equation that corresponds to this slope field must be 0 when the same values are plugged into both variables. Also, for $y < x$, $\frac{dy}{dx}$ must be positive, since the slopes are positive. For $y > x$, $\frac{dy}{dx}$ must be negative, since the slopes are negative.

5. **CORRECT ANSWER: A**

   Incorrect answer comments, same for all 4:

   The slopes in the slope field change when either the x-value changes or y-value changes. So the differential equation that corresponds to this slope field contains both variables. Also, the slopes in the slope field are 0 when $x = 0$, and undefined when $y = 0$. Also, when both variables are the same sign, $\frac{dy}{dx}$ must be negative, since the slopes are negative. When the variables are opposing signs, $\frac{dy}{dx}$ must be positive, since the slopes are positive.

DIFFICULTY LEVEL 2

6. **CORRECT ANSWER: E**

   Incorrect answer comments, same for all 4:

   Take the derivative using Implicit Differentiation, which says take the derivative of x and y as if they were separate functions. Whenever the derivative of a y term is taken, the result is $\frac{dy}{dx}$. For this example, the derivate is $3x(\frac{dy}{dx}) + 3y - 2y(\frac{dy}{dx}) = 2$. Solve for $\frac{dy}{dx}$ and evaluate at the given point.

7. **CORRECT ANSWER: E**

   Incorrect answer comments, same for all 4:

   Take the derivative using Implicit Differentiation, which says take the derivative of x and y as if they were separate functions. Whenever the derivative of a y term is taken, the result is $\frac{dy}{dx}$. Remember to use the Product Rule when taking the derivative of the term xy. Solve for $\frac{dy}{dx}$.

8. **CORRECT ANSWER: B**

   Incorrect answer comments, same for all 4:

   Take the derivative using Implicit Differentiation, which says take the derivative of x and y as if they were separate functions. Whenever the derivative of a y term is taken, the result is $\frac{dy}{dx}$. For this example, the derivate is $2x(\frac{dy}{dx}) + 2y - 2y(\frac{dy}{dx}) = 0$. Solve for $\frac{dy}{dx}$. In order to find the x-value to plug into the derivative, plug in y = 1 into the equation of the curve and solve for x. Plug both coordinates into the derivative.

9. **CORRECT ANSWER: C**

   Incorrect answer comments, same for all 4:

   Take the derivative using Implicit Differentiation, which says take the derivative of x and y as if they were separate functions. Whenever the derivative of a y term is taken, the result is $\frac{dy}{dx}$. For this example, the derivate is $y^2 + 2xy(\frac{dy}{dx}) + 6(\frac{dy}{dx}) = 10$. Solve for $\frac{dy}{dx}$. In order to find the y-value to plug into the derivative, plug in x = 2 into the equation of the curve and solve for y in the first quadrant. Plug both coordinates into the derivative.

10. **CORRECT ANSWER: B**

    Incorrect answer comments, same for all 4:

    Take the derivative using Implicit Differentiation, which says take the derivative of x and y as if they were separate functions. Whenever the derivative of a y term is taken, the result is $\frac{dy}{dx}$. After taking the derivative, solve for $\frac{dy}{dx}$. Plug in the coordinates into the derivative and find the slope.

11. CORRECT ANSWER: C

Incorrect answer comments, same for all 4:

Take the derivative using Implicit Differentiation, which says take the derivative of x and y as if they were separate functions. Whenever the derivative of a y term is taken, the result is $\frac{dy}{dx}$. Solve for $\frac{dy}{dx}$. Plug both coordinates into the derivative to find the slope. Last, write out the equation of a line in point-slope form with the information substituted in.

12. CORRECT ANSWER: A

Incorrect answer comments, same for all 4:

Take the second derivative using Implicit Differentiation. Remember to apply the Quotient Rule. When the term $\frac{dy}{dx}$ reappears, plug in the earlier result, $\frac{-y}{4y+x}$. Evaluate the second derivative at the given coordinates.

13. CORRECT ANSWER: C

Incorrect answer comments, same for all 4:

Take the derivative using Implicit Differentiation, and solve for $\frac{dy}{dx}$. Take the derivative of $\frac{dy}{dx}$ and solve for $\frac{d^2y}{dx^2}$. Evaluate both derivatives at the given point. Remember that a graph is increasing when the derivative is positive, and decreasing when its derivative is negative. A graph is concave up when the second derivative is positive, and concave down when its second derivative is negative.

14. CORRECT ANSWER: E

Incorrect answer comments, same for all 4:

The slopes in the slope field are 0 when $x = 0$. Determine which solutions have a derivative of 0 when $x = 0$. Also, for $x > 0$, $\frac{dy}{dx}$ must be positive, since the slopes are positive. For $x < 0$, $\frac{dy}{dx}$ must be negative, since the slopes are negative. Finally, determine which solution can be drawn into the slope field, so that the curve of the solutions following the lines in the slope field.

15. **CORRECT ANSWER: D**

   Incorrect answer comments, same for all 4:

   The slopes in the slope field are 0 when $x = 0$. Determine which solutions have a derivative of 0 when $x = 0$. Also, for $x < 0$, $\frac{dy}{dx}$ must be positive, since the slopes are positive. For $x > 0$, $\frac{dy}{dx}$ must be negative, since the slopes are negative. Determine which solutions are increasing when $x < 0$ and decreasing when $x > 0$.

16. **CORRECT ANSWER: A**

   Incorrect answer comments, same for all 4:

   The given differential equation is equal to 0 when $y = -2x$. Determine which slope field has slopes of 0 at only those points.

17. **CORRECT ANSWER: A**

   Incorrect answer comments, same for all 4:

   The given differential equation is never equal to 0. Also, for all x-values, it is positive, which means the slopes on the slope field should be positive. Determine which slope field has corresponding information.

DIFFICULTY LEVEL 3

18. **CORRECT ANSWER: B**

   Incorrect answer comments, same for all 4:

   Take the derivative using Implicit Differentiation, which says take the derivative of x and y as if they were separate functions. Whenever the derivative of a y term is taken, the result is $\frac{dy}{dx}$. After taking the derivative, solve for $\frac{dy}{dx}$. Replace any variables of y with an equivalent expression in terms of x and simplify.

19. **CORRECT ANSWER: D**

   Incorrect answer comments, same for all 4:

Take the derivative using Implicit Differentiation, which says take the derivative of x and y as if they were separate functions. Whenever the derivative of a y term is taken, the result is $\frac{dy}{dx}$. Solve for $\frac{dy}{dx}$. Horizontal tangent lines occur when the derivative is equal to 0, so find the y-values that make the derivative zero. Last, plug this y-value into the equation of the curve to find the x-value.

20. CORRECT ANSWER: D

Incorrect answer comments, same for all 4:

Take the derivative using Implicit Differentiation, and solve for $\frac{dy}{dx}$. For this example, the derivate is $\frac{dy}{dx} = \frac{-2x}{y}$. Take the derivative of $\frac{dy}{dx}$ and when the term $\frac{dy}{dx}$ appears, plug in the earlier result, $\frac{-2x}{y}$. Evaluate the second derivative at the given coordinates.

21. CORRECT ANSWER: B

Incorrect answer comments, same for all 4:

Take the derivative using Implicit Differentiation, and solve for $\frac{dy}{dx}$. For this example, the derivate is $\frac{dy}{dx} = \frac{-x}{y}$. Take the derivative of $\frac{dy}{dx}$ and when the term $\frac{dy}{dx}$ appears, plug in the earlier result, $\frac{-x}{y}$. After simplifying the second derivative, the term $x^2 + y^2$ will appear. Replace with substitution using the original equation.

THE FOUR THEOREMS (EXTRA)

DIFFICULTY LEVEL 1

1. **CORRECT ANSWER: A**

   Incorrect answer comments, same for all 4:

   The Extreme Value Theorem states that all continuous functions on a closed interval have at least one minimum and maximum value. Determine which condition of the EVT this function fails.

2. **CORRECT ANSWER: D**

   Incorrect answer comments, same for all 4:

   (F) The Intermediate Value Theorem states that for a continuous function on a closed interval, if $f(a) = A$ and $f(b) = B$, then for every x-value between a and b, the graph has to reach every y-value between A and Essentially, if the graph hits y-values of 10 and -5, it must reach every number in between. Find the value of a which ensures the graph will pass through $y = -\dfrac{3}{4}$ twice.

3. **CORRECT ANSWER: E**

   Incorrect answer comments, same for all 4:

   (G) The Intermediate Value Theorem states that for a continuous function on a closed interval, if $f(a) = A$ and $f(b) = B$, then for every x-value between a and b, the graph has to reach every y-value between A and Essentially, if the graph hits y-values of 10 and -5, it must reach every number in between. Find the value of k which ensures the graph will pass through $y = 7$ twice.

4. **CORRECT ANSWER: C**

   Incorrect answer comments, same for all 4:

   Rolle's Theorem states that for all differentiable functions on a closed interval, if two points share the same y-value, then for some c between them, $f'(c) = 0$. This theorem only works on continuous and differentiable functions. Determine which condition is not being met.

DIFFICULTY LEVEL 2

5. **CORRECT ANSWER: C**

   Incorrect answer comments, same for all 4:

   Based on the Intermediate Value Theorem for choices I and III, look at the y-values the function hits and determine if that means it would also have to hit 0 or 8. Based on the Extreme Value Theorem for choice II, all continuous functions on a closed interval have at least one minimum value. Determine if those conditions are met.

6. **CORRECT ANSWER: B**

   Incorrect answer comments, same for all 4:

   The Mean Value Theorem states that for all differentiable functions on a closed interval, the slope between any two points is equal to the slope at c, a point between the two endpoints. Find the slope between the endpoints, and set that equal to the derivative. Find the x-value and plug it into $f(x)$ to find the y-value.

7. **CORRECT ANSWER: B**

   Incorrect answer comments, same for all 4:

   The Mean Value Theorem states that for all differentiable functions on a closed interval, the slope between any two points is equal to the slope at c, a point between the two endpoints. Find the slope between the endpoints, and set that equal to the derivative. Solve for x.

8. **CORRECT ANSWER: E**

   Incorrect answer comments, same for all 4:

   The Mean Value Theorem states that for all differentiable functions on a closed interval, the slope between any two points is equal to the slope at c, a point between the two endpoints. Find the slope between the endpoints, and set that equal to the derivative. Solve for x, and remember that the values for the MVT must be between the endpoints.

9. **CORRECT ANSWER: D**

   Incorrect answer comments, same for all 4:

The Mean Value Theorem requires differentiable functions in order to apply. The graph of g is not differentiable at $x = 0$, so the MVY cannot apply to any x-values greater than $x = 0$.

10. CORRECT ANSWER: E

Incorrect answer comments, same for all 4:

For choice I, the minimum of the 5 given values of f is 7, but without a graph or equation, it is impossible to tell the minimum for f overall. Based on Rolle's Theorem for choice II, the function is continuous and differentiable. Why can we guarantee that our function has two equal y-values, even though it is not evident in the table? Based on the Intermediate Value Theorem for choice III, observe the function between 4 and 6, and between 6 and 8 to see if the function reaches $f(x) = 10$ twice.

11. CORRECT ANSWER: E

Incorrect answer comments, same for all 4:

Since f is continuous and differentiable on a closed interval, the Intermediate, Extreme, and Mean Value Theorem all apply. Only Rolle's Theorem has the extra condition where $f(0) = f(5)$ for the derivative at a point in the interval to be equal to 0.

DIFFICULTY LEVEL 3

12. CORRECT ANSWER: D

Incorrect answer comments, same for all 4:

Rolle's Theorem states that for all differentiable functions on a closed interval, if two points share the same y-value, then for some c between them, $h'(t) = 0$. Observe the number of times the values in the table change from increasing to decreasing or vice versa. Each time will result in the function passing through the same y-value, resulting in another time $h'(t) = 0$.

13. CORRECT ANSWER: E

Incorrect answer comments, same for all 4:

Since f is continuous and differentiable on a closed interval, the Intermediate, Extreme, and Mean Value Theorem all apply. For choice I, apply the Intermediate Value Theorem to determine if the function must pass through the given y-value. For choice II, if the end points are the same y-value, apply Rolle's Theorem to determine if the derivative must be 0 at a point. For choice III, apply the Mean Value Theorem to find the slope between the endpoints and determine if the derivative must be equal to that slope.

INTERPRETATIONS AND PROPERTIES OF DEFINITE INTEGRALS

DIFFICULTY LEVEL 1

1. **CORRECT ANSWER: C**

   Incorrect answer comments, same for all 4:

   Take the antiderivative to get $\int_{1}^{2}(6x^2-5)dx = (2x^3-5x)\Big|_{1}^{2}$. Evaluate the antiderivative at $x = 2$ and $x = 1$, and subtract the results.

2. **CORRECT ANSWER: A**

   Incorrect answer comments, same for all 4:

   Rewrite the expression as $(2x^{-3})$ and then take the antiderivative. Evaluate the antiderivative at $x = 2$ and $x = 1$, and subtract the results.

3. **CORRECT ANSWER: E**

   Incorrect answer comments, same for all 4:

   The net change in position is found using a definite integral of velocity. Find the antiderivative of velocity, $\int_{2}^{3} v(t)dt = p(3) - p(2)$, to find the change in starting and ending position, or displacement.

4. **CORRECT ANSWER: A**

   Incorrect answer comments, same for all 4:

   Even functions are symmetric around the y-axis. So $\int_{-1}^{1} f(x)dx = 2\int_{0}^{1} f(x)dx = -2\int_{-1}^{0} f(x)dx$

5. **CORRECT ANSWER: D**

   Incorrect answer comments, same for all 4:

   Take the antiderivative and evaluate at t = x and t = 0, and subtract the results.

6. **CORRECT ANSWER: D**

   Incorrect answer comments, same for all 4:

   When taking the antiderivative, followed by taking the derivative, the operations result in returning the original expression, with the variable x substituted in for t. The lower limit is irrelevant, the process of taking the derivative eliminates the value of 0 evaluated in the antiderivative.

DIFFICULTY LEVEL 2

7. **CORRECT ANSWER: B**

   Incorrect answer comments, same for all 4:

   Expand the expression $(2x-1)^2$ and then take the antiderivative. Evaluate the antiderivative at x = 0 and x = -1, and subtract the results.

8. **CORRECT ANSWER: C**

   Incorrect answer comments, same for all 4:

   To find the area under the curve of a function, we use a definite integral. Simplify the expression and take the antiderivative to get $\int_{1}^{2}(2x+\frac{1}{x})dx = (x^2 + \ln|x|)\Big|_{1}^{2}$. Evaluate the antiderivative at x = 2 and x = 1, and subtract the results.

9. **CORRECT ANSWER: D**

   Incorrect answer comments, same for all 4:

   Take the antiderivative to get $\int_{-2}^{a} x\,dx = \frac{x^2}{2}\Big|_{-2}^{a} = 0$. Evaluate the antiderivative at x = a and x = -2, and subtract the results. Solve the equation for a.

10. CORRECT ANSWER: C

Incorrect answer comments, same for all 4:

Take the antiderivative to get $\int_{\frac{\pi}{2}}^{\pi}(\cos t + k)\,dt = \sin t + kt\Big|_{\frac{\pi}{2}}^{\pi} = 3\pi - 1$. Evaluate the antiderivative at $t = \pi$ and $t = \frac{\pi}{2}$, and subtract the results. Solve the equation for k.

11. CORRECT ANSWER: A

Incorrect answer comments, same for all 4:

The integral $\int_{1}^{3} f(x)\,dx$ finds the signed area under the graph of f. The length of the interval $[1,3]$ gives the width of the area, and the height of the graph gives the height of the area. Since the width is 2, find the possible heights using the range of f, and find the maximum and minimum area under the curve using the product of width and height.

12. CORRECT ANSWER: C

Incorrect answer comments, same for all 4:

Take the antiderivative of each term separately. Substitute in $(2k-3)$ in for the first integral. Evaluate the second integral at $x = k$ and $x = 1$, and subtract the results. Add together the results from both integrals.

13. CORRECT ANSWER: B

Incorrect answer comments, same for all 4:

Switching the upper and lower limits of the second integral negates it so that $\int_{2}^{100} f(x)dx + \int_{100}^{1} f(x)dx = \int_{2}^{100} f(x)dx - \int_{1}^{100} f(x)dx$. Separate the second integral into two smaller integrals so that

$$\int_{2}^{100} f(x)dx - \int_{1}^{100} f(x)dx =$$

$\int_{2}^{100} f(x)dx - \left(\int_{1}^{2} f(x)dx + \int_{2}^{100} f(x)dx \right)$. Cancel out the common integrals and reduce.

14. CORRECT ANSWER: E

Incorrect answer comments, same for all 4:

$$\int_{0}^{5} g(x)dx =$$

$\int_{0}^{3} g(x)dx + \int_{3}^{5} g(x)dx$. Switching the upper and lower limits of the last integral negates it, so that both known values of the integrals can be substituted in. Solve for $\int_{0}^{3} g(x)dx$

15. CORRECT ANSWER: C

Incorrect answer comments, same for all 4:

Use U-Substitution, and let $U = t^2$. Taking the derivative of U and solving for dx yields $dx = \dfrac{dU}{2t}$. Substitution into the integral of the new variables gives $\dfrac{1}{2}\int_{0}^{x} e^{U} dU$. Take the antiderivative, replace the value of U, evaluate at t = x and t = 0, and subtract the results.

16. CORRECT ANSWER: A

Incorrect answer comments, same for all 4:

When taking the antiderivative, followed by taking the derivative, the operations result in returning the original expression, with the variable x substituted in for t. Since the lower limit is x, the original expression will be negative. The upper limit is irrelevant, the process of taking the derivative eliminates the value of 2 evaluated in the antiderivative.

17. **CORRECT ANSWER: C**

    Incorrect answer comments, same for all 4:

    When taking the antiderivative, followed by taking the derivative, the operations result in returning the original expression, with the variable x substituted in for t. Plug in x = 2 into the original expression, $\dfrac{2}{1+t^3}$.

18. **CORRECT ANSWER: E**

    Incorrect answer comments, same for all 4:

    The function f is increasing when f' is positive. $f'(x) = \dfrac{d}{dx}\int_0^x (t-1)e^t \, =(x-1)e^x$. Find where $f'(x) = 0$, then plug in x-values on either side of the zeroes to see where the derivative is positive (increasing).

19. **CORRECT ANSWER: C**

    Incorrect answer comments, same for all 4:

    For the accumulation function, $g(x) = \int_2^x f(t)dt$, $g(a)$ = the area under the curve between x = -2 and x = a. If the curve is above the x-axis, the area is positive, and if the curve is below the x-axis, the area is negative. If a<-2, the the signs for area above and below the curve are reversed.

DIFFICULTY LEVEL 3

20. CORRECT ANSWER: A

Incorrect answer comments, same for all 4:

Integrating the rate of change of temperature gives the current temperature, so $\int_0^4 2e^{2t}dt = T(4) - T(0)$. Evaluate the integral, substitute in the known temperature, and solve for $T(4)$

21. CORRECT ANSWER: D

Incorrect answer comments, same for all 4:

When taking the antiderivative, followed by taking the derivative, the operations result in returning the original expression. So, if $f(t) = \cos(t^3 + 1)$ and $F(t) = \int \cos(t^3 + 1)dt$, then $\int_0^{x^2} \cos(t^3 + 1)dt = F(x^2) - F(0)$. When taking the derivative, $\frac{d}{dx}\int_0^{x^2} \cos(t^3 + 1)dt = \frac{d}{dx}(F(x^2) - F(0)) = f(x^2) \bullet 2x$. Simply put, plug the upper limit x^2 into the original expression, and multiply by the derivative of x^2 due to the Chain Rule. The lower limit is irrelevant, the process of taking the derivative eliminates the value of 0 evaluated in the antiderivative.

22. CORRECT ANSWER: B

Incorrect answer comments, same for all 4:

Functions have a point of inflection when the second derivate changes sign. Take the second derivate of $g(x) = \int_0^x f(t)dt$, which results in $g''(x) = f'(x)$. Notice where $f'(x)$ changes sign, which is where the slope of the graph of f changes sign.

APPLICATIONS OF INTEGRALS

DIFFICULTY LEVEL 1

1. **CORRECT ANSWER: E**

   Incorrect answer comments, same for all 4:

   The definite integral of a function gives the signed area under the curve. Find the area of each region between the curve and the x-axis. If the area lies above the axis, the value is positive, and if the area lies below the axis, the value is negative.

2. **CORRECT ANSWER: C**

   Incorrect answer comments, same for all 4:

   The area between two curves is given by the equation $Area = \int_a^b (f(x) - g(x))dx$, where $f(x)$ is the upper function, and $g(x)$ is the lower function. Also, a is the lower limit, the x-value where the area begins, and b is the lower limit, the x-value where the area ends. By setting the functions equal, we solve for x to get $a = -2$ and $b = 2$. Drawing a sketch of the graphs is important to determine the limits, and to determine that $y = 7$ is the upper function, and $y = x^2 + 3$ is the lower function. Finally, evaluate the integral of $Area = \int_{-2}^{2}(7-(x^2+3))dx = \int_{-2}^{2}(4-x^2)dx$ to find the area.

3. **CORRECT ANSWER: B**

   Incorrect answer comments, same for all 4:

   The area between two curves is given by the equation $Area = \int_j^k (u(x) - l(x))dx$, where $u(x)$ is the upper function, and $l(x)$ is the lower function. Also, j is the lower limit, the x-value where the area begins, and k is the lower limit, the x-value where the area ends. Here, $f(x)$ is the upper function, and $g(x)$ is the lower function. The location of the x-axis is irrelevant for the area between curves.

4. **CORRECT ANSWER: A**

   Incorrect answer comments, same for all 4:

   The average value of a function from $[a, b]$ is $\dfrac{1}{b-a}\int_a^b f(x)\,dx$. Remember that the antiderivative of $\sec^2 x$ is $\tan x$.

5. **CORRECT ANSWER: D**

   Incorrect answer comments, same for all 4:

   The average value of a function from $[a, b]$ is $\dfrac{1}{b-a}\int_a^b f(x)\,dx$. Integrate this expression and use the evaluation theorem to find the average value.

DIFFICULTY LEVEL 2

6. **CORRECT ANSWER: A**

   Incorrect answer comments, same for all 4:

   The area between two curves is given by the equation $Area = \int_a^b (f(x) - g(x))\,dx$, where $f(x)$ is the upper function, and $g(x)$ is the lower function. Also, a is the lower limit, the x-value where the area begins, and b is the lower limit, the x-value where the area ends. By setting the functions equal, we solve for x to get $a = 1$ and $b = 5$. Drawing a sketch of the graphs is important to determine the limits, and to determine that $y = 2x$ is the upper function, and $y = x^2 - 4x + 5$ is the lower function. Finally, evaluate the integral of $Area = \int_1^5 (2x - (x^2 - 4x + 5))\,dx = \int_1^5 (-x^2 + 4x - 5)\,dx$ to find the area.

7. **CORRECT ANSWER: C**

   Incorrect answer comments, same for all 4:

   The area between two curves is given by the equation $Area = \int_a^b (f(x) - g(x))\,dx$, where $f(x)$ is the upper function, and $g(x)$ is the lower function. Also, a is the lower limit, the x-value where the area begins, and b is the lower limit, the x-value where the area ends. The limits are given in the form of the lines, so $a=1$ and $b=e$. Drawing a sketch of the graphs is important to determine the limits, and to determine that $y=\frac{1}{x}$ is the upper function, and the x-axis, $y=0$, is the lower function. Finally, evaluate the integral of $Area = \int_{1}^{e} \frac{1}{x} dx$ to find the area.

8. **CORRECT ANSWER: B**

Incorrect answer comments, same for all 4:

The volume of an area rotated around one of its boundaries creates disk-shaped cross-sections. The formula for this is given by $Volume = \pi \int_{a}^{b} R^2 dx$, where R is distance from the far side of the region to the axis of revolution. Here, $R = x-0 = x$, since the axis of revolution is the x-axis. Also, a is the lower limit, the x-value where the area begins, and b is the lower limit, the x-value where the area ends. Drawing a sketch of the graphs is important to determine the limits. Evaluate the integral of $Volume = \pi \int_{0}^{2} x^2 dx=$ to find the volume.

9. **CORRECT ANSWER: A**

   Incorrect answer comments, same for all 4:

   The volume of a solid with rectangular cross-sections is given by $Volume = k\int_a^b f(x)^2\,dx$, where k is ratio of the height to the width of the rectangles.. Here, $f(x) = \sqrt{x}$ and $k = 5$. Also, a is the lower limit, the x-value where the area begins, and b is the lower limit, the x-value where the area ends. Evaluate the integral of $Volume = 5\int_0^4 (\sqrt{x})^2\,dx$ to find the volume.

10. **CORRECT ANSWER: E**

    Incorrect answer comments, same for all 4:

    The average value of a function from $[a, b]$ is $\dfrac{1}{b-a}\int_a^b f(x)\,dx$. Integrate this expression and use the evaluation theorem to find the average value. Remember when integrating, $\int e^{ax}\,dx = \dfrac{e^{ax}}{a}$.

DIFFICULTY LEVEL 3

11. **CORRECT ANSWER: C**

    Incorrect answer comments, same for all 4:

    Since both graphs are horizontally oriented, it is preferable to the area using y and a variable instead of x. The area between two curves is given by the equation $Area = \int_a^b (f(y) - g(y))\,dy$, where $f(y)$ is the right-most function, and $g(y)$ is the left-most function. Also, a is the lower limit, the y-value where the area begins, and b is the lower limit, the y-value where the area ends. By setting the functions equal, we solve for y to get $a = -2$ and $b = 2$. Determine the right-most and left-most function, and substitute the functions and limits into the area equation.

12. **CORRECT ANSWER: C**

    Incorrect answer comments, same for all 4:

The area beneath a curve is given by the equation $Area = \int_a^b f(x)\,dx$. Since k divides R into two equal regions, then $\int_0^k \sqrt{x}\,dx = \int_k^1 \sqrt{x}\,dx$. Integrate both sides of the equation, and solve for the variable k.

13. **CORRECT ANSWER: C**

    Incorrect answer comments, same for all 4:

    The volume of an area rotated around one of its boundaries creates disk-shaped cross-sections. The formula for this is given by $Volume = \pi \int_a^b R^2\,dx$, where R is distance from the far side of the region to the axis of revolution. Here, $R = (x^2 + 6) - 4 = x^2 + 2$, since the axis of revolution is $y = 4$. Also, a is the lower limit, the x-value where the area begins, and b is the lower limit, the x-value where the area ends.

14. **CORRECT ANSWER: A**

    Incorrect answer comments, same for all 4:

    The volume of an area rotated around a separate axis creates washer-shaped cross-sections. The formula for this is given by $Volume = \pi \int_a^b (R^2 - r^2)\,dx$, where R is distance from the far side of the region to the axis of revolution and r is the distance from the near side of the region to the axis of revolution. Here, $R = 2 - \frac{1}{x^2}$ and $r = 2 - 1 = 1$ since the axis of revolution is $y = 2$.

    Also, a is the lower limit, the x-value where the area begins, and b is the lower limit, the x-value where the area ends.

15. **CORRECT ANSWER: C**

    Incorrect answer comments, same for all 4:

    The volume of an area rotated around one of its boundaries creates disk-shaped cross-sections. Since the axis of revolution is vertical, the integral is in terms of y and the formula for this is given by $Volume = \pi \int_a^b R^2\,dy$, where R is distance from the far side of the region to the axis of revolution. Here, $R = \frac{y}{2} - 0 = \frac{y}{2}$, since the axis of revolution is the y-axis. Also, a is the lower limit, the y-value where the area begins, and b is the lower limit, the y-value where the area ends.

16. **CORRECT ANSWER: D**

    Incorrect answer comments, same for all 4:

    The volume of an area rotated around one of its boundaries creates disk-shaped cross-sections. Since the axis of revolution is vertical, the integral is in terms of y and the formula for this is given by $Volume = \pi \int_a^b (R^2 - r^2) dy$, where R is distance from the far side of the region to the axis of revolution and r is the distance from the near side of the region to the axis of revolution. Here, $R = 4 - 0 = 4$ and $r = y^2 - 0 = y^2$ since the axis of revolution is the y-axis. Also, a is the lower limit, the y-value where the area begins, and b is the lower limit, the y-value where the area ends. Drawing a sketch of the graphs is important to determine the limits. Evaluate the integral of $Volume = \pi \int_0^2 ((4)^2 - (y^2)^2) dy$ to find the volume.

17. **CORRECT ANSWER: D**

    Incorrect answer comments, same for all 4:

    Integrating the rate of change in a value gives the total sum. So to find the number of people on line, the evaluation theorem states $\int_a^b p(t) dt = P(b) - P(a)$ where $P(x)$ is the total number of people on line at a given time. Since it is known that $P(0) = 30$, substitute in the given values into the integral and solve for $P(3)$.

TECHNIQUES OF ANTIDIFFERENTIATION

DIFFICULTY LEVEL 1

1. **CORRECT ANSWER: A**

   Incorrect answer comments, same for all 4:

   Use the basic rules for integration of Trigonometric Functions.

2. **CORRECT ANSWER: D**

   Incorrect answer comments, same for all 4:

   Use the basic rules for integration of Inverse Trigonometric Functions.

3. **CORRECT ANSWER: E**

   Incorrect answer comments, same for all 4:

   $\int \cos(ax)\,dx = \dfrac{\sin(ax)}{a}$. Take the antiderivative, evaluate at $x = \dfrac{\pi}{6}$ and $x = 0$, and subtract the results.

4. **CORRECT ANSWER: E**

   Incorrect answer comments, same for all 4:

   $\int e^{ax}\,dx = \dfrac{e^{ax}}{a}$. Take the antiderivative, evaluate at $x = 4$ and $x = 2$, and subtract the results.

5. **CORRECT ANSWER: D**

   Incorrect answer comments, same for all 4:

   Take the derivative of U and solve for dx to get $dx = \dfrac{dU}{5}$. Substitute both U and dx into the integral. Also, plug the limits of integration, $x = -1$ and $x = 2$, into $U = 5x + 6$ to rewrite the limits in terms of U.

6. **CORRECT ANSWER: B**

   Incorrect answer comments, same for all 4:

   Use U-Substitution, and let $U = x+2$. Taking the derivative of U and solving for dx yields $dx = dU$. Substitution into the integral of the new variables, and substitution of the limits, gives $\int_{3}^{7} f(U)dU$. The use of x or U as the variable in the function is irrelevant, so $\int_{3}^{7} f(U)dU = \int_{3}^{7} f(x)dx$.

DIFFICULTY LEVEL 2

7. **CORRECT ANSWER: A**

   Incorrect answer comments, same for all 4:

   Simplify the integral so that $\int \frac{x\sec^2 x - 1}{x} dx = \int \left(\sec^2 x - \frac{1}{x} \right) dx$. Use the basic rules for integration of Trigonometric Functions and Logarithmic Functions.

8. **CORRECT ANSWER: B**

   Incorrect answer comments, same for all 4:

   Use U-Substitution, and let $U = \tan \theta$. Taking the derivative of U and solving for $d\theta$ yields $d\theta = \frac{dU}{\sec^2 \theta}$. Substitution into the integral of the new variables gives $\int \frac{1}{U} dU$. Take the antiderivative, replace the value of U, evaluate at $\theta = \frac{\pi}{3}$ and $\theta = \frac{\pi}{4}$, and subtract the results.

9. **CORRECT ANSWER: C**

   Incorrect answer comments, same for all 4:

   To integrate $f'(x)$, use U-Substitution, and let $U = x^3$. Taking the derivative of U and solving for dx yields $dx = \frac{dU}{3x^2}$. Substitution into the integral of the new variables gives $\int \frac{1}{3} e^U dU$. Take the antiderivative and replace the value of U.

10. **CORRECT ANSWER: A**

   Incorrect answer comments, same for all 4:

   Use U-Substitution, and let $U = 3 - x^2$. Taking the derivative of U and solving for dx yields $dx = \dfrac{dU}{-2x}$. Substitution into the integral of the new variables gives $-3\int \dfrac{1}{\sqrt{U}}\, dU$. Take the antiderivative and replace the value of U.

DIFFICULTY LEVEL 3

11. **CORRECT ANSWER: D**

   Incorrect answer comments, same for all 4:

   Use U-Substitution, and let $U = \sin x$. Taking the derivative of U and solving for dx yields $dx = \dfrac{dU}{\cos x} = \sec x\, dU$. Substitution into the integral of the new variables gives $\int e^U\, dU$. Take the antiderivative, replace the value of U, evaluate at $x = k$ and $x = 0$, and subtract the results. Set this difference equal to $\left(\sqrt{e} - 1\right)$ and solve for k.

APPLICATIONS OF ANTIDIFFERENTIATION

DIFFICULTY LEVEL 1

1. **CORRECT ANSWER: E**

   Incorrect answer comments, same for all 4:

   (H) Take the antiderivative of the velocity to get the position. The result, $x(t) = \int(-4t+15)dt = -2t^2 + 15t + C$, has a constant term, Plug in the initial conditions, $x = -5$ when $t = 1$, and solve for C. Then evaluate $x(3)$.

2. **CORRECT ANSWER: B**

   Incorrect answer comments, same for all 4:

   (I) Take the antiderivative of the acceleration to get the velocity. The result, $v(t) = \int(2\sin t - 5)dt = -2\cos t - 5t + C$, has a constant term, Plug in the initial conditions, $v = \pi$ when $t = 0$, and solve for C. Then evaluate $v\left(\dfrac{\pi}{3}\right)$.

DIFFICULTY LEVEL 2

3. **CORRECT ANSWER: A**

   Incorrect answer comments, same for all 4:

   Take the antiderivative of the acceleration to get the velocity. The result has a constant term, C_1. Plug in the initial conditions, $v = -1$ when $t = 2$, and solve for C_1. Take the antiderivative again to get the position. The result has a different constant term, C_2. Plug in the initial conditions, $p = 5$ when $t = 2$, and solve for C_1.

4. **CORRECT ANSWER: D**

   Incorrect answer comments, same for all 4:

   Take the antiderivative of the acceleration to get the velocity. The result has a constant term, C_1. Plug in the initial conditions, $v = -0.5$ when $t = 1$, and solve for C_1. Take the antiderivative again to get the position. The result has a different constant term, C_2, which cannot be solved for. Evaluate $p(3) - p(1)$ and simplify.

5. **CORRECT ANSWER: A**

   Incorrect answer comments, same for all 4:

   Take the antiderivative of the velocity to get the position. The result has a constant term, C. Plug in the initial conditions, $p = -9$ when $t = 4$, and solve for C. Also, solve for when the velocity equation is equal to 0, to determine that the bug changes direction at $t = 3$. Find the position of the bug at $t = 0$, $t = 3$ and $t = 4$. Add the absolute value of the difference in position for both intervals to get the total distance.

6. **CORRECT ANSWER: C**

   Incorrect answer comments, same for all 4:

   When given a graph of velocity, the area under the curve represents the directed distance. The integral $\int_{2}^{7} v(t)\,dt = p(7) - p(2)$ can be solved for $p(7)$. Plug in the value of $p(2)$, and find the value of $\int_{2}^{7} v(t)\,dt$ by finding the signed area under the curve, positive if it is above the axis, and negative if it is below.

7. **CORRECT ANSWER: C**

   Incorrect answer comments, same for all 4:

   When given a graph of velocity, the area under the curve represents the directed distance. The integral $\int_{0}^{5} |v(t)\,dt|$ will give the total distance traveled. Find the signed area under the curve, and remember to take the absolute value of find the distance.

8. **CORRECT ANSWER: B**

   Incorrect answer comments, same for all 4:

   Separate the variables to get $\dfrac{dy}{y} = 6\,dx$. Then integrate each side to get $\ln y = 6x + c$. Solving for y results in $y = e^{6x+c} = C_2 e^{6x}$. This substitution of variables is possible using the laws of exponentials. Then plug in the initial conditions and solve for the constant.

9. **CORRECT ANSWER: C**

   Incorrect answer comments, same for all 4:

   Separate the variables and integrate each side of the equation. Plug in the initial conditions and solve for the constant. Then, find y when $x=0$, and evaluate the differential equation at this value.

10. **CORRECT ANSWER: C**

    Incorrect answer comments, same for all 4:

    Rewrite the original equation as $\frac{dy}{dx} = ky$. Separate the variables and integrate each side of the equation. Plug in the first initial conditions and solve for the constant. Plug in the second initial conditions and solve for k.

DIFFICULTY LEVEL 3

11. **CORRECT ANSWER: B**

    Incorrect answer comments, same for all 4:

    Separate the variables to get $y\,dy = 3x^2\,dx$. Then integrate each side to get $\frac{y^2}{2} = x^3 + c$. Solve for c using the initial conditions. Then evaluate the equation at $y=16$ and solve for x.

12. **CORRECT ANSWER: E**

    Incorrect answer comments, same for all 4:

    Integrate the given differential expression and plug in the initial conditions to solve for the constant. Then evaluate the equation at $t=3$.

13. **CORRECT ANSWER: C**

    Incorrect answer comments, same for all 4:

    Write out the differential equation $\frac{dV}{dt} = k\sqrt{V}$. Separate the variables and integrate each side of the equation. Plug in the first initial conditions and solve for the constant c. Plug in the second initial conditions and solve for k.

NUMERICAL APPROXIMATIONS TO DEFINITE INTEGRALS

DIFFICULTY LEVEL 1

1. **CORRECT ANSWER: E**

   Incorrect answer comments, same for all 4:

   The area using a Right Riemann Sum is given by $A=(x_2-x_1)\bullet f(x_2)+(x_3-x_2)\bullet f(x_3)...$ where each product is the area of a rectangle in each subinterval. Here, the width of each of the rectangles is 2, and the height of each rectangle is the value of f at $x = 4, 6,$ and 8, respectively.

2. **CORRECT ANSWER: B**

   Incorrect answer comments, same for all 4:

   The area using a Left Riemann Sum is given by $A=(x_2-x_1)\bullet f(x_1)+(x_3-x_2)\bullet f(x_2)...$ where each product is the area of a rectangle in each subinterval. Here, the width of each of the rectangles is 1, and the height of each rectangle is the value of f at $x = 0, 1,$ and 2, respectively.

3. **CORRECT ANSWER: A**

   Incorrect answer comments, same for all 4:

   The area using a Midpoint Riemann Sum is given by $A=(x_2-x_1)\bullet f(\frac{x_1+x_2}{2})+(x_3-x_2)\bullet f(\frac{x_2+x_3}{2})...$ where each product is the area of a rectangle in each subinterval. Here, the width of each of the rectangles is 2, and the height of each rectangle is the value of f at $x = 1, 3,$ and 5, respectively.

4. CORRECT ANSWER: C

Incorrect answer comments, same for all 4:

Distance is the antiderivative of velocity. Find the area under the curve of velocity using a Left Riemann Sum is given by $A = (x_2 - x_1) \cdot f(x_1) + (x_3 - x_2) \cdot f(x_2)\ldots$ where each product is the area of a rectangle in each subinterval. Here, the width of each of the rectangles is 5, and the height of each rectangle is the value of f at t = 0, 5, and 10, respectively. This is distance the train travels, plus the original position, which was 12 feet.

DIFFICULTY LEVEL 2

5. CORRECT ANSWER: D

Incorrect answer comments, same for all 4:

The area using a Trapezoidal Riemann Sum is given by $A = (x_2 - x_1) \cdot \dfrac{f(x_1) + f(x_2)}{2} + (x_3 - x_2) \cdot \dfrac{f(x_2) + f(x_3)}{2}\ldots$ where each product is the area of a trapezoid in each subinterval. Here, the width of each of the trapezoids is 2, 1, and 4, and the height of each trapezoid is average of the two y-values.

6. CORRECT ANSWER: C

Incorrect answer comments, same for all 4:

The area using a Left Riemann Sum is given by $A = (x_2 - x_1) \cdot f(x_1) + (x_3 - x_2) \cdot f(x_2)\ldots$ and the area using a Right Riemann Sum is given by $A = (x_2 - x_1) \cdot f(x_2) + (x_3 - x_2) \cdot f(x_3)\ldots$ where each product is the area of a rectangle in each subinterval. For both, find the approximation and subtract the results.

7. CORRECT ANSWER: D

Incorrect answer comments, same for all 4:

Separate the area to be approximated into three intervals. From [0, 4] and [12, 16], either a Left or Right Riemann Sum will be a close approximation. From [4, 12], a Trapezoidal Riemann Sum with 2 subintervals will more closely follow the curve. Add up the result of each approximation.

8. **CORRECT ANSWER: A**

   Incorrect answer comments, same for all 4:

   Sketch a picture of any increasing and concave up function. Draw in the corresponding rectangles and trapezoids for the Riemann Sum process. Determine which of the Riemann Sums has its objects strictly underneath the curve, thus underestimating the area.

DIFFICULTY LEVEL 3

9. **CORRECT ANSWER: C**

   Incorrect answer comments, same for all 4:

   Find the x-values that make the function equal to 0. Then, determine which approximation method uses those x-values in its area summation.

10. **CORRECT ANSWER: B**

    Incorrect answer comments, same for all 4:

    The area using a Trapezoidal Riemann Sum for this question is given by $18.5 = (k-1) \cdot \frac{18+16}{2} + (2-k) \cdot \frac{20+18}{2}$. Solve the equation for k.

11. **CORRECT ANSWER: D**

    Incorrect answer comments, same for all 4:

    The area using a Midpoint Riemann Sum is given by $A = (x_2 - x_1) \cdot f(\frac{x_1 + x_2}{2}) + (x_3 - x_2) \cdot f(\frac{x_2 + x_3}{2})\ldots$ where each product is the area of a rectangle in each subinterval. Here, the width of each of the rectangles is 1, and the height of each rectangle is the value of f at $x = \frac{3}{2}$ and $\frac{5}{2}$, respectively. Subtract this approximation from the value of $\int_{1}^{3} \frac{1}{x^2} dx$.

12. CORRECT ANSWER: B

Incorrect answer comments, same for all 4:

The $\frac{1}{4}$ coefficient represents the width of each rectangular subinterval, not a coefficient of the original integral. Since there are four terms inside, there are a total of four subintervals, so the interval is 1 unit wide. Since the remaining choices all have intervals from [0, 1], the numbers being evaluated cannot be larger than 1. Determine which integral fits all of these criteria.

Made in the USA
San Bernardino, CA
17 August 2017